11+ Full Length Practice Tests

By

John Smith

ABOUT THE PRACTICE TESTS

- This book contains 4 tests, Set A (Paper 1 + Paper 2) and Set B (Paper 1 + Paper 2).
- The tests are based on CEM pattern and closely follow the topics and style of questions that have appeared in the recent past.
- These tests may be taken in the write-in format or the multiple-choice format.
- For the write-in format, the answers can be marked on the paper itself.
- For multiple-choice format, the answer can be marked by drawing a horizontal pencil line through the correct box.
- Answer Sheets and Explanations are provided. These may be cut out before you start doing the test.

TIMING

- One of the most important element of the tests is time management.
- These tests are split into individually timed sections and the time allocated is clearly marked in the beginning of the section.
- Please ensure that the time limit for _each section_ is strictly adhered to.

SCORE

- Each Question has equal weightage and carries 1 mark.
- You should aim for a score of at least 75%.

SET A: PAPER 1

There are 3 Sections in this examination:

Section 1: Verbal Reasoning – Cloze

Section 2: Numerical Reasoning

Section 3: Non - Verbal Reasoning

<u>Note:</u> **This exam has a total of 82 questions (including parts of multi-part questions)**

SECTION 1: VERBAL REASONING – CLOZE

YOU HAVE 6 MINUTES TO COMPLETE THIS SECTION

THERE ARE 16 QUESTIONS IN THIS SECTION

Many animals in the wild are suspicious and fearful

①
- ☐ at
- ☐ to
- ☐ in
- ☐ of

human beings.

②
- ☐ collect
- ☐ take
- ☐ eat
- ☐ put

These animals _____ flight instantly when a human approaches.

③
- ☐ soon
- ☐ early
- ☐ late
- ☐ not

Man, however, _____ discovered that some animals

④
- ☐ should
- ☐ would
- ☐ shall
- ☐ could

⑤
- ☐ Unlike
- ☐ Despite
- ☐ Dislike
- ☐ Like

be tamed or domesticated. _____ animals in the wild, these animals

⑥
- ☐ should
- ☐ would
- ☐ may
- ☐ can

allow man to come close to them. They

⑦
- ☐ should
- ☐ would
- ☐ may
- ☐ can

⑧
- ☐ them
- ☐ their
- ☐ there
- ☐ these

even allow ... owners to stroke or pet

⑨
- ☐ them
- ☐ their
- ☐ there
- ☐ these

. Back

⑩
- ☐ in
- ☐ to
- ☐ by
- ☐ with

the olden days, man

⑪
- ☐ should
- ☐ would
- ☐ may
- ☐ can

domesticate animals

⑫
- ☐ towards
- ☐ into
- ☐ by
- ☐ for

setting traps to catch

⑬
- ☐ them
- ☐ their
- ☐ there
- ☐ these

young ones.

A young animal is far more easily domesticated

⑭
- ☐ than
- ☐ then
- ☐ from
- ☐ by

an adult

one. From young age, the animal learns

⑮
- ☐ at
- ☐ to
- ☐ in
- ☐ of

trust and obey

⑯
- ☐ its
- ☐ it's
- ☐ to
- ☐ it is

owner.

SECTION 2: NUMERICAL REASONING

YOU HAVE 25 MINUTES TO COMPLETE THIS SECTION

THERE ARE 9 MULTI-PART QUESTIONS IN THIS SECTION

(1) There are a total of 500 balls in a box. 75% of the balls are red, 10 balls are blue, 1% are yellow, and the rest are black.

a) How many red balls are there in the box?

_____

b) What percentage of the total balls in the box is blue?

_____ %

c) How many balls in the box are yellow?

_____

d) How many balls in the box are black?

_____

e) What percentage of the balls in the box is black?

_____ %

② Two fair coins are tossed.

a) What is the probability that we get HEADS on both turns?

$\frac{1}{4}$ □ $\frac{1}{2}$ □ $\frac{2}{3}$ □ $\frac{1}{3}$ □ 1 □

b) What is the probability of getting one HEADS and one TAILS?

$\frac{1}{2}$ □ $\frac{1}{4}$ □ $\frac{1}{6}$ □ $\frac{1}{8}$ □ 1 □

A third coin is tossed simultaneously with the first two.

c) What is the probability of getting three TAILS?

$\frac{1}{9}$ □ $\frac{1}{8}$ □ 1 □ $\frac{1}{3}$ □ $\frac{3}{5}$ □

d) What is the probability of getting three HEADS?

$\frac{1}{9}$ □ $\frac{1}{8}$ □ 1 □ $\frac{1}{3}$ □ $\frac{3}{5}$ □

③ Consider the figure box shown below. (NOT TO SCALE)

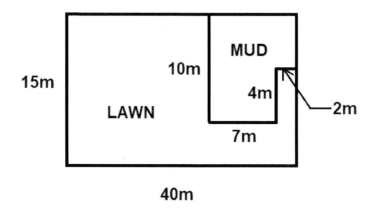

a) What is the area of the MUD in m²?

_____ m²

b) What is the area of the LAWN in m² ?

_____ m²

c) What is the volume of soil excavated in m³ if 1m deep digging is done in the whole area of the MUD?

_____ m³

d) A fence is to be put up throughout the boundary of the LAWN and the MUD area, including the division between the two areas. What is the length of this fence?

_____ m

(4) A person is stranded in the desert. He aimlessly tries to find the way by moving in random directions.

```
        N
        |
W ------+------ E
        |
        S
```

a) The person walks 300m from his original position to the North, then 500m to the South-East direction, and finally 400m to the West. How far is he from his original position?

100m	0m	1200m	500m	400m
☐	☐	☐	☐	☐

b) The person starts walking from his original position towards West. After walking 200m, he turns to his left and walks another 200m. Then again, he turns left and walks 200m. Where and how far is he from his original position?

200m to the South	200m to the East	0m	100m to the North
☐	☐	☐	☐

c) The person, starting from the original point, goes 100m to the North, turns left and walks another 100m, turns right and walks 200m, turns right and walks 100m. Where is he now with respect to his original position?

300m to the South	300m to the North	At his original position	100m to the West
☐	☐	☐	☐

(5) A shop sells a certain brand of pens. The individual cost of the pen is £0.75. However, following incentives are given:

£1.50 for 3 pens

£2.00 for 5 pens

£2.50 for 10 pens

a) What is the price per pen if 10 pens are bought?

£ _____

b) What is the price per pen if 5 pens are bought?

£ _____

c) What would be the total price of 10 pens if no incentives are given?

£ _____

d) What would be the minimum total price of 15 pens with the given incentives?

£ _____

e) What would be the total price of 20 pens without any incentives?

£ _____

6 The graph shows the positions of different people.

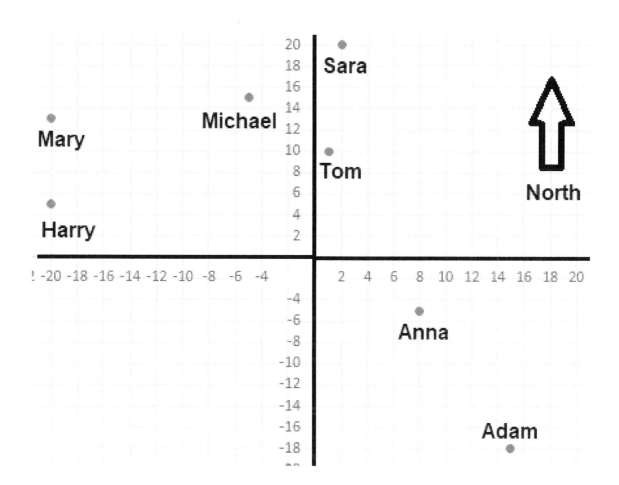

a) What are the coordinates of Michael?

(14,16)	(-4,-6)	(15,5)	(-5,15)	(-5,-15)
☐	☐	☐	☐	☐

b) What are the coordinates of Harry?

(20,5)	(5,20)	(5,-20)	(-20,5)	(-20,-5)
☐	☐	☐	☐	☐

c) Anna walks 15 units to the north, and 7 units to the west. Where is she now?

Tom's place   Sara's place   At a random point   At origin   Harry's place

☐   ☐   ☐   ☐   ☐

Consider that people can only move on the grid lines (only in vertical and horizontal directions).

d) Which two persons are the farthest from each other?

Adam-Sara   Adam-Harry   Adam-Mary   Adam-Michael

☐   ☐   ☐   ☐

e) Which two persons are closest to each other?

Tom-Sara   Tom-Michael   Harry-Mary   Adam-Anna

☐   ☐   ☐   ☐

7 The pie chart below shows 4 different fruits. The total number of fruits is 1000.

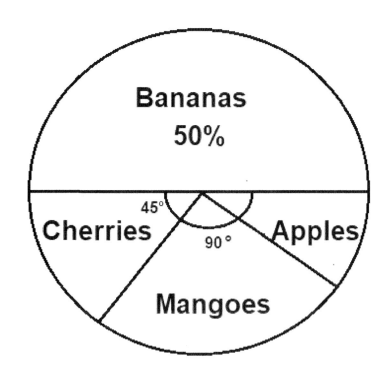

a) How many Cherries are there?

_____

b) How many apples are there?

_____

c) What percentage of the total fruits is mangoes?

_____ %

d) How many bananas are there?

_____

8 A father is thrice as old as his son. In 20 years, the father will be twice as old as his son.

a) What is the current age of the father?

_____ years

b) What is the current age of the son?

_____ years

9 A clock shows the current time to be 9:00.

a) How many degrees will the minute-needle travel clockwise when the time is 9:15?

360 degrees	180 degrees	90 degrees	45 degrees
☐	☐	☐	☐

b) How many degrees will the hour-needle travel clockwise in 12 hours?

360 degrees   180 degrees   90 degrees   45 degrees

☐   ☐   ☐   ☐

c) What would be the time if the minute-needle travels 720 degrees clockwise?

11:00   12:00   11:30   12:30

☐   ☐   ☐   ☐

d) What would be the time if the hour-needle travels 90 degrees?

11:00   12:00   11:30   12:30

☐   ☐   ☐   ☐

SECTION 3: NON - VERBAL REASONING

YOU HAVE 14 MINUTES TO COMPLETE THIS SECTION

THERE ARE 28 QUESTIONS IN THIS SECTION

Choose the shape on the right that fits the question mark in the large square on the left to complete the pattern.

①

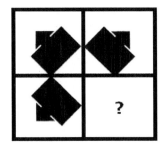 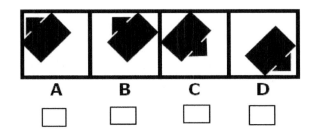

②

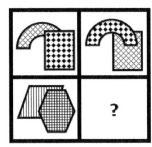 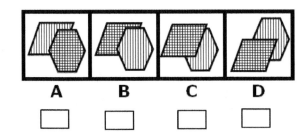

③

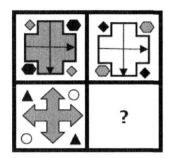 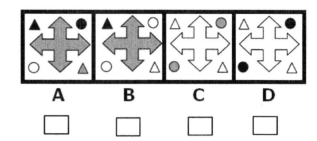

A   B   C   D

④

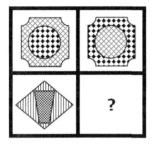 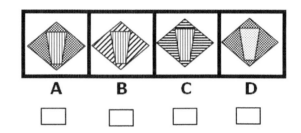

A   B   C   D

⑤

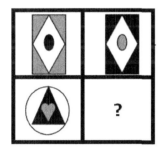 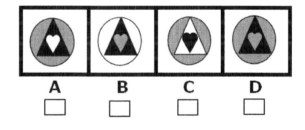

A   B   C   D

⑥

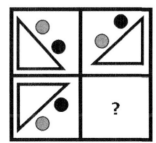 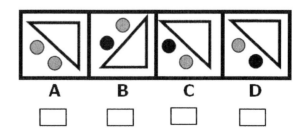

A   B   C   D

⑦

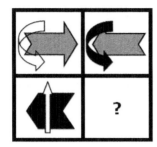 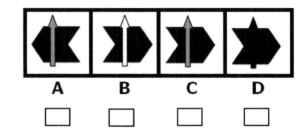

⑧

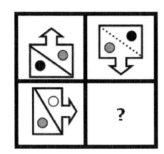 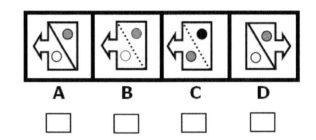

⑨

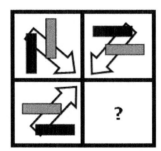 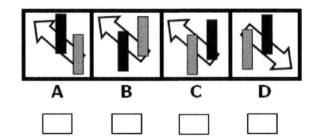

⑩

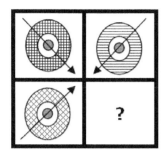 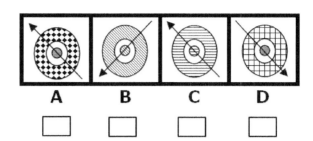

A B C D

⑪

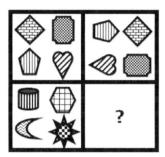 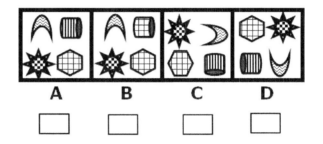

A B C D

FIND THE ODD ONE OUT.

⑫

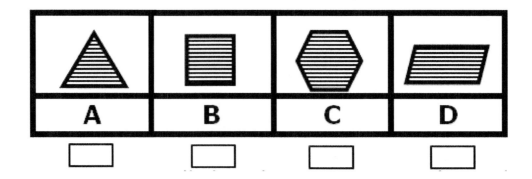

⑬

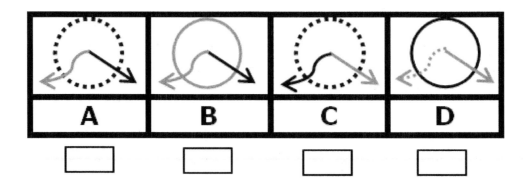

⑭

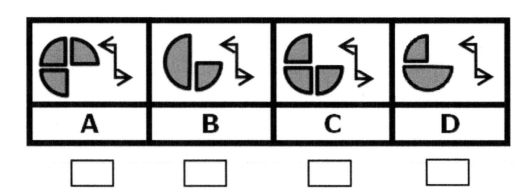

⑮

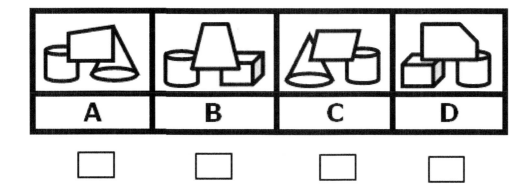

A	B	C	D

☐   ☐   ☐   ☐

⑯

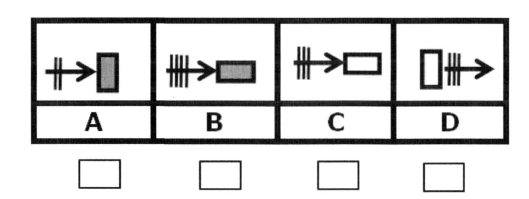

A	B	C	D

☐   ☐   ☐   ☐

⑰

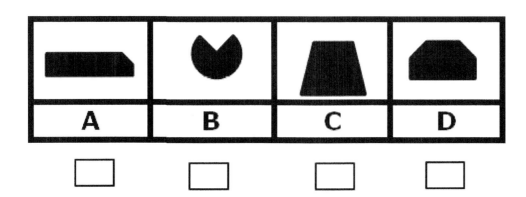

A	B	C	D

☐   ☐   ☐   ☐

⑱

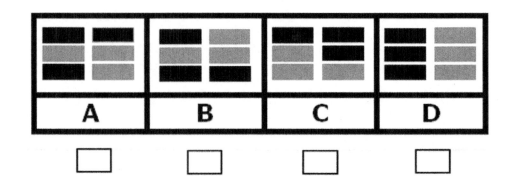

⑲

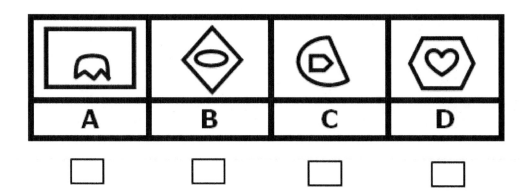

⑳

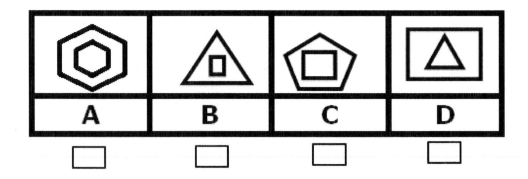

㉑

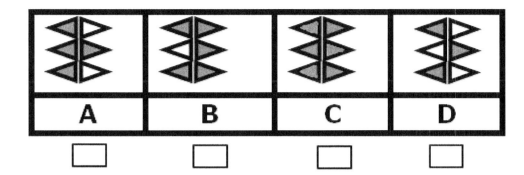

A	B	C	D
☐	☐	☐	☐

㉒

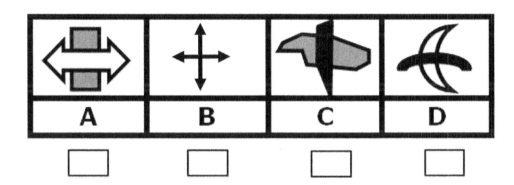

A	B	C	D
☐	☐	☐	☐

Select which shape accurately shows the top-view of the 3d shape:

㉓

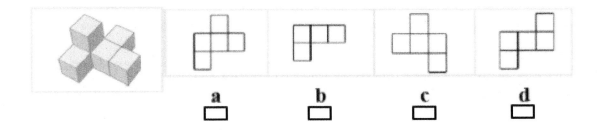

a ☐ b ☐ c ☐ d ☐

㉔

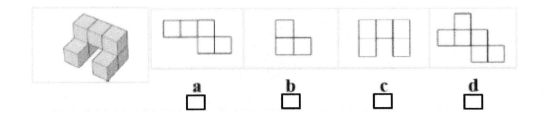

a ☐ b ☐ c ☐ d ☐

㉕

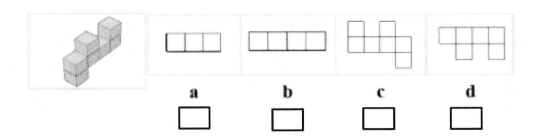

a ☐ b ☐ c ☐ d ☐

㉖

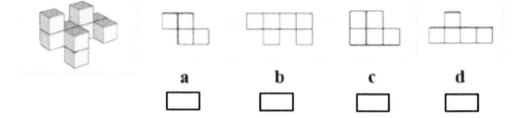

a
☐

b
☐

c
☐

d
☐

㉗

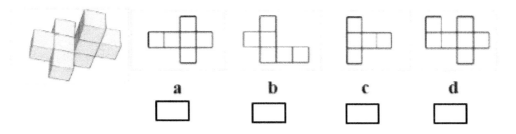

a
☐

b
☐

c
☐

d
☐

㉘

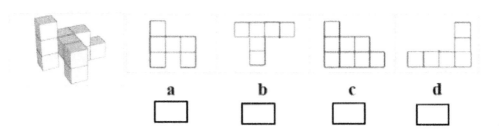

a
☐

b
☐

c
☐

d
☐

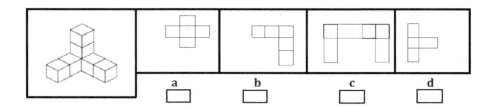

a   b   c   d

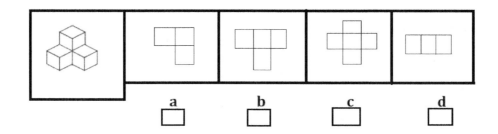

a   b   c   d

THE END

SET A: PAPER 2

There are 6 Sections in this examination:

Section 1: Verbal Reasoning – Comprehension 1

Section 2: Verbal Reasoning – Comprehension 2

Section 3: Verbal Reasoning – Multiple Meanings

Section 4: Verbal Reasoning – Antonyms

Section 5: Verbal Reasoning – Synonyms

Section 6: Numerical Reasoning

<u>Note:</u> **This Paper has a total of 95 questions**

SECTION 1: VERBAL REASONING – COMPREHENSION 1

YOU HAVE 12 MINUTES TO COMPLETE THIS SECTION

READ THE PASSAGE CAREULLY AND ANSWER THE QUESTIONS THAT FOLLOW

THERE ARE 16 QUESTIONS IN THIS SECTION

A terrible scream –- a prolonged yell of horror and anguish burst out of the silence of the *moor. That frightful cry turned the blood to ice in my veins. "Oh my God!" I gasped. "What is it? What does it mean?"

Sherlock Holmes sprang to his feet, and I saw his dark, athletic outline at the door of the hut, his
5   shoulders stooping, his head thrust forward, his face peering into the darkness.

"Hush!" he whispered. "Hush!"

The cry had been loud on account of its intensity, but it had pealed out from somewhere far off on the shadowy plain. Now it burst upon our ears, nearer, louder, and more urgent than before. "Where is it?" Holmes whispered; and I knew from the thrill of his voice that he, the man of iron, was shaken to the
10   soul. "Where is it, Watson?"

"There I think," I pointed into the darkness.

"No, there!"

Again, the agonised cry swept through the silent night, louder and much nearer than ever. And a new sound mingled with it, a deep, muttered roar, musical and yet menacing, rising and falling like the low,
15   constant murmur of the sea.

"The hound!" cried Holmes, "Come, Watson, come! Good heavens if we are too late!"

He had started running swiftly over the moor, and I had followed at his heels.

But now from somewhere among the broken ground immediately in front of us there came one last despairing yell and then a dull, heavy thud. We halted and listened. Not another sound broke the heavy silence of the windless night.

Blindly we ran through the gloom, blundering against rocks, forcing our way through bushes, panting up hills and rushing down slopes, heading always in the direction whence those dreadful sounds had come. At every rise Holmes looked eagerly round him, but the shadows were thick upon the moor and nothing moved upon its dreary face.

"Can you see anything? "Nothing." "But hark, what is that?"

A low moan had fallen upon our ears. There it was again upon our left! On that side a ridge of rocks ended in a sheer cliff which overlooked a stone-strewn slope. On its jagged face was spread-eagled some dark, irregular object. As we ran towards it, the vague outline hardened into a definite shape. It was a prostrate man face downward upon the ground, the head doubled under him at a horrible angle, the shoulders rounded, and the body hunched together as if in the act of throwing a somersault. The moan had been the passing of his soul.

Source: Adapted from The Hounds of the Baskervilles by Sir Arthur Conan Doyle

* moor: a tract of open land

① The story starts with the phrase, 'a terrible scream'. The purpose of beginning the story with this phrase is to

    A- incite a climax
    B- introduce a character
    C- describe a sub-plot
    D- introduce the overall setting

② Which two words from the text are CLOSEST in meaning?

    A- Jagged , Irregular
    B- Swept, Thud
    C- Gloom, Gasp
    D- Sprang, Peering

③ The phrase, 'his shoulders stooping, his head thrust forward, his face peering into the darkness' (line 5) indicates Sherlock Holmes's

    A- Keen interest
    B- Shock and weakness
    C- Decision to ignore his fear
    D- Fright at hearing the loud yell

④ The description of Holmes in the passage BEST supports that he was

    A- Alert and curious
    B- Athletic and inactive
    C- Shaken due to shock
    D- Not concerned about safety of others

⑤ Which quality of the detective is emphasized by the phrase 'the man of iron'   (lines 9-10)?

    A- Profoundness
    B- Strength of wit
    C- Steadfastness and honesty
    D- Physical and mental strength

(6) Which set of words BEST relates to sounds?

    A- Yell, moan, cry
    B- Gasp, pealed, horror
    C- Whisper, yell, gloom
    D- Gasp, horror, scream

(7) "Blindly we ran through the gloom, <u>blundering</u> against rocks, <u>forcing</u> our way through bushes, <u>panting</u> up hills and rushing down slopes."

The underlined words BEST support the fact that Holmes and Watson were

    A- Running passionately
    B- Trying to stay ahead of each other
    C- Struggling while chasing the sound
    D- Helping each other during the chase

(8) The story MAINLY focuses on

    A- The intensity of sound
    B- Four characters and their problems
    C- The personality of Sherlock Holmes
    D- How the detective chased the sound

(9) At the end of the passage, the description of the dying man MOST likely indicates that

    A- his death was the result of extreme violence
    B- his appearance was different than Holmes
    C- he used to live near the moor
    D- he was crushed under a rock

(10) The overall tone of the narrator shows

    A- nervousness
    B- calmness
    C- thrill
    D- fear

(11) Which option best describes the meaning of the word 'swiftly' (line 17) as used in the passage?

    A- quickly
    B- scaringly
    C- slowly
    D- carefully

(12) What is the meaning of the word "hound"?

    A- nervousness
    B- calmness
    C- wolf
    D- hunting dog

(13) "The hound!" cried Holmes' (line 16) expresses that Holmes:

    A- started crying out of fear
    B- shouted loudly
    C- was very calm
    D- spoke very confidently

(14) In which paragraph it became clear that a person has been killed?

    A- First paragraph
    B- Second Paragraph
    C- Last paragraph
    D- We cannot say for sure that he was killed

(15) What is CLOSEST in meaning to the word "hark" (line 27) ?

    A- buddy
    B- hey
    C- listen
    D- none of the above

(16) What is CLOSEST in meaning to the word "somersault" (line 30) ?

    A- An acrobatic act
    B- Running
    C- Swift movement
    D- Slow movement

SECTION 2: VERBAL REASONING – COMPREHENSION 2

YOU HAVE 8 MINUTES TO COMPLETE THIS SECTION

READ THE PASSAGE CAREULLY AND ANSWER THE QUESTIONS THAT FOLLOW

THERE ARE 10 QUESTIONS IN THIS SECTION

It was dark still, but there was enough light to see by. Light on pandemonium it was. Nature can put on a thrilling show. The stage is vast, the lighting is dramatic, the extras are innumerable, and the budget for special effects is absolutely unlimited. What I had before me was a spectacle of wind and water, an earthquake of the senses that even Hollywood could not orchestrate. But the earthquake stopped at the ground beneath my feet. The ground beneath my feet was solid. I was a spectator safely ensconced in his seat.

It was when I looked up at a lifeboat on the bridge castle that I started to worry. The lifeboat was not hanging straight down. It was leaning in from its davits. I turned and looked at my hands. My knuckles were white. The thing was, I was not holding on so tightly because of the weather, but because otherwise I would fall in towards the ship. The ship was listing to port, to the other side. It was not a severe list, but enough to surprise me. When I looked overboard the drop was not sheer any more. I could see the ship's great black side.

A shiver of cold went through me. I decided it was a storm after all. Time to return to safety. I let go, hotfooted it to the wall, moved over and pulled open the door.

Inside the ship, there were noises. Deep structural groans. I stumbled and fell. No harm done. I got up. With the help of the handrails I went down the stairwell four steps at a time. I had gone down just one level when I saw water. Lots of water. It was blocking my way. It was surging from below like a riotous crowd, raging, frothing, and boiling. Stairs vanished into watery darkness. I could not believe my eyes.

20 What was this water doing here? Where had it come from? I stood nailed to the spot, frightened and incredulous and ignorant of what I should do next. Down there was where my family was.

I ran up the stairs. I got to the main deck. The weather was not entertaining any more. I was very afraid. And it was not level the other way either. There was a noticeable incline going from bow to stern. I looked overboard. The water did not look to be eighty feet away. The ship was sinking. My mind could hardly conceive it. It was as unbelievable as the moon catching fire.

25 Where were the officers and the crew? What were they doing? Towards the bow I saw some men running in the gloom. I thought I saw some animals too, but I dismissed the sight as illusion crafted by rain and shadow. We had the hatch covers over their bay pulled open when the weather was good, but at all times the animals were kept confined to their cages. These were dangerous wild animals we were transporting, not farm livestock. Above me, on the bridge, I thought I heard some men shouting. The 30 ship shook and there was that sound, the monstrous metallic burp. What was it? Was it the collective scream of humans and animals protesting their oncoming death? Was it the ship itself giving up the ghost? I fell over. I got to my feet. I looked overboard again. The sea was rising. The waves were getting closer. We were sinking fast.

Source: Adapted from The Life of Pi by Yann Martel

① In paragraph 1, the narrator compares nature and Hollywood films in order to

    A- describe that art is present in nature
    B- discuss the earthquake that was about to come
    C- highlight the dramatic effect of changing scenes
    D- explain his feelings about the films he recently watched

② 'An earthquake of the senses' in line 4 indicates the narrator's

    A- emotions at witnessing nature's might
    B- confusion at witnessing a mighty storm
    C- concern to save himself from the severity of weather
    D- emphasis on describing why he felt calm despite the storm

③ The word 'orchestrate' (line 4) is CLOSEST in meaning to

    A- desire
    B- accept
    C- imagine
    D- demonstrate

④ In paragraph 2 (line 9), why were the narrator's knuckles white?

    A- He was feeling very cold
    B- He was scared
    C- He was wearing gloves for a long time
    D- He was holding onto the ship very tightly

⑤ The purpose of paragraph 2 is to

    A- Describe the ship
    B- Sketch narrator's feelings
    C- Build anticipation of the coming storm
    D- Discuss narrator's concerns about his family

⑥ Which expression MOST vividly indicates the narrator's fears?

    A- Deep structural groans
    B- A shiver of cold went through me
    C- Now it was plain and obvious: the ship was listing badly
    D- It was when I looked up at a lifeboat on the bridge that I started to worry

⑦ The words 'nagging, frothing, and boiling' (line 18) are used to describe the

    A- Storm outside the ship
    B- Uncontrolled rush of water
    C- Atmosphere experienced by the ship's crew
    D- Severity of weather experienced by the narrator

⑧ The phrases 'like a riotous crowd' (line 18) and 'unbelievable as the moon catching fire' (line 26) are indicative of the comparisons the narrator has made to describe what he experienced.

The MOST likely reason for using these comparisons is to demonstrate the

    A- Impact and severity of his feelings
    B- Rhythm created through those words
    C- Severity of weather he has experienced
    D- Positivity required to cope with difficult situations

⑨ The narrator first realised that the ship could be sinking in line

    A- 5
    B- 10
    C- 23
    D- 27

⑩ "I stood nailed to the spot" (line 19) means that the narrator was

    A- Using tools to save others
    B- Unable to move due to shock
    C- Waiting for the ship crew at a spot
    D- Doubtful whether he should move or not

SECTION 3: VERBAL REASONING – MULTIPLE MEANINGS

YOU HAVE 4 MINUTES TO COMPLETE THIS SECTION

THERE ARE 12 QUESTIONS IN THIS SECTION

Choose the word which has a similar meaning to the words in both sets of brackets

① (SMOOTH, LEVEL) _____ (APARTMENT, MAISONETTE)

Plane	Even	Flat	Mansion
☐	☐	☐	☐

② (SPAN, SCOPE) _____ (VARIETY, COLLECTION)

Scale	Reach	Trivia	Range
☐	☐	☐	☐

③ (CRUEL, NASTY) _____ (INTEND, PLAN)

Vicious	Plot	Mean	Propose
☐	☐	☐	☐

④ (HAMMER, HIT) _____ (THROB, PULSATE)

Mallet	Nail	Smack	Pound
☐	☐	☐	☐

⑤ (DELICATE, FEATHERY) _____ (BRIGHT, SUNLIT)

Light	Flimsy	Downy	Clever
☐	☐	☐	☐

⑥ (IRIS, LENS) _____ (APPRENTICE, STUDENT)

Eye	Pupil	University	Class
☐	☐	☐	☐

⑦ (LETTER, MESSAGE) _____ (OBSERVE, SEE)

Communication	Note	Moral	Spot
☐	☐	☐	☐

⑧ (TOLERATE, ALLOW) _____ (CARRY, SUPPORT)

Bear	Stand	Lug	Ear
☐	☐	☐	☐

⑨ (COMPLAIN, OPPOSE) _____ (ITEM, THING)

Grumble	Noun	Object	Fight
☐	☐	☐	☐

⑩ (STARVE, ABSTAIN) _____ (QUICK, RAPID)

Hunger	Speedy	Waterfall	Fast
☐	☐	☐	☐

⑪ (STRENGTH, POWER) _____ (MAY, COULD)

Force	Might	Possibly	April
☐	☐	☐	☐

⑫ (JUST, HONEST) _____ (AVERAGE, SATISFACTORY)

Just	Fair	Only	Beautiful
☐	☐	☐	☐

SECTION 4: VERBAL REASONING – ANTONYMS

YOU HAVE 6 MINUTES TO COMPLETE THIS SECTION

THERE ARE 16 QUESTIONS IN THIS SECTION

Complete the word on the right so that it means the opposite, or nearly the opposite, of the word on the left.

① Foremost

u	n		m	p					t

② Beautiful

u	g		

③ Modern

a	n		i			

④ Divided

u	n		t		

⑤ Superiority

	n							y

(6) Natural

| a | r | | | | i | c | | |

(7) Strict

| l | | n | | e | n | |

(8) Trivial

| s | e | | i | o | |

(9) Mobile

| f | | x | | |

(10) Convict

| a | | q | | | t |

(11) Never

| a | l | | | | |

(12) Practical

| t | h | | o | r | t | | | l |

(13) Married

| | a | | h | e | | | |

(14) Professional

a	m		t			

(15) Bitter

s		e		

(16) Bright

	u		

SECTION 5: VERBAL REASONING – SYNONYMS

YOU HAVE 6 MINUTES TO COMPLETE THIS SECTION

THERE ARE 18 QUESTIONS IN THIS SECTION

Complete the word which means the same, or nearly the same, as the word on the left.

①	**ERRONEOUS**	Wrong ☐	Enormous ☐	Weak ☐	Eroded ☐
②	**SEIZE**	Start ☐	Release ☐	Length ☐	Grasp ☐
③	**ARTIFICIAL**	Natural ☐	Synthetic ☐	Solid ☐	Beautiful ☐
④	**FABLE**	Truth ☐	Story ☐	Return ☐	Restoration ☐
⑤	**SERENE**	Tranquil ☐	Renounce ☐	Deny ☐	Possess ☐

⑥ EXPAND	Convert ☐	Condense ☐	Congest ☐	Swell ☐
⑦ MORTAL	Immortal ☐	Divine ☐	Perishable ☐	Spiritual ☐
⑧ LAUNCH	Invest ☐	Inaugurate ☐	Relinquish ☐	Prepare ☐
⑨ FRAUDULENT	Candid ☐	Genuine ☐	Original ☐	Swindling ☐
⑩ STARTLED	Finished ☐	Relaxed ☐	Endless ☐	Astonished ☐
⑪ FRESH	Faulty ☐	Sluggish ☐	Disgraceful ☐	New ☐
⑫ RAVISHING	Pretty ☐	Ugly ☐	Weak ☐	Responsible ☐
⑬ AWARE	Uncertain ☐	Ignorant ☐	Doubtful ☐	Sure ☐

⑭ **SHRINK**   Contract   Stretch   Spoil   Expand

　　　　　　　　☐　　　　　☐　　　　☐　　　☐

⑮ **COMMON**   Rare   Small   Petty   Usual

　　　　　　　　☐　　　☐　　　☐　　　☐

⑯ **COMFORT**   Uncomfort   Miscomfort   Discomfort   None of these

　　　　　　　　☐　　　　　☐　　　　　☐　　　　☐

⑰ **EVASIVE**   Free   Honest   Liberal   Ambiguous

　　　　　　　　☐　　　☐　　　☐　　　☐

⑱ **GREGARIOUS**   Unfriendly   Glorious   Horrendous   Social

　　　　　　　　☐　　　☐　　　☐　　　☐

SECTION 6: NUMERICAL REASONING

YOU HAVE 9 MINUTES TO COMPLETE THIS SECTION

THERE ARE 23 QUESTIONS IN THIS SECTION

① What is the percentage increase of 70 to 140?

_____ %

② What is the percentage decrease of 1200 to 300?

_____ %

③ Tom's gas bill is £24. It increased by 12% after 12 months. A further 25% increase is applied six months later. What is Tom's gas bill after 18 months?

£ _____

④ Jay walks at 10 Km/h for 3 hours and then at 4 km/h for 9 hours. Katy walks at a constant speed. If they both walk the same distance, and take the same time, what is Katy's speed of walking?

_____ Km/hour

Information for Questions 5 and 6

A cyclist travels 10km in first 20 minutes, 1000m in next 5 minutes, and 400,000 cm in further 5 minutes.

(5) What is the total distance covered by the cyclist?

_____ Km

(6) What is his average speed for the journey?

_____ Km/h

(7) The ratio between the speeds of two trains is 8 : 7. If the first train runs 440 kms in 4 hours, then the speed of the second train is train is:

_____ Km/h

(8) 40% of a number is 20. What is the number?

_____

(9) What ratio is 12 minutes to one hour?

_____

(10) How many seconds are there in 1/4th of 6 hours?

_____ seconds

(11) The 4th February of a leap year is Monday. What day is it on 4th of March of the same year?

Monday   Tuesday   Thursday   Saturday

☐   ☐   ☐   ☐

(12) A window-sill is at the height of 80 feet. The foot of the ladder must be placed 15 feet from the wall. What is the area of the triangle formed by the ladder, wall and the ground?

_____ feet^2

(13) A pupil is standing at 12th place from the right, and 9th place from the left. How many pupils are there in the row?

19   20   21   22

☐   ☐   ☐   ☐

(14) A square and a rectangle have the same perimeter (40 m). If the length of the rectangle is 3 times its width, what is difference between the area of the square and the rectangle?

_____ m^2

⑮ If the answer to the previous question is represented as a square, what would be the length of its side?

    6 m   5 m   1.25 m   2.5 m

    ☐   ☐   ☐   ☐

⑯ A father is 30 years older than his son. He will be thrice as old as his son in 5 years. How old is the son currently?

_____ years

⑰ The area of right-angled triangle with height 8m and base 4m is:

_____ m^2

⑱ Find the next number in sequence: 1, 2, 4, 8, 16, 32, …….

    64   48   128   44

    ☐   ☐   ☐   ☐

⑲ Out of a total of 100 students, 50 students passed in Physics and 70 passed in Chemistry, 5 students failed in both the subjects. How many students passed in both the subjects?

    30   50   25   15

    ☐   ☐   ☐   ☐

20 A kitchen has enough food for 500 people for 10 days. How long will the food last if 4500 more people join to eat?

1 day	5 days	half day	2 days
☐	☐	☐	☐

21 Paul eats a certain percentage of cake in an hour. He continues eating the same amount of cake every hour and finishes the whole cake in 5 hours. What percentage of cake does he eat every hour?

5%	10%	20%	50%
☐	☐	☐	☐

22 Find the next number in sequence: 1 , 4, 9, 16, 25, ...

30	34	36	49
☐	☐	☐	☐

23 Find the next number in sequence: 2, 3, 5, 7, 11, ...

15	13	14	17
☐	☐	☐	☐

THE END

SET B: PAPER 1

There are 5 sections in this examination:

Section 1: Verbal Reasoning – Comprehension

Section 2: Verbal Reasoning – Cloze

Section 3: Verbal Reasoning – Odd One Out

Section 4: Verbal Reasoning – Antonyms

Section 5: Non-Verbal Reasoning

<u>Note:</u> The exam has a total of 95 questions

SECTION 1: VERBAL REASONING – COMPREHENSION

YOU HAVE 15 MINUTES TO COMPLETE THIS SECTION

READ THE PASSAGE CAREULLY AND ANSWER THE QUESTIONS THAT FOLLOW

THERE ARE 20 QUESTIONS IN THIS SECTION

Once upon a time there was a royal elephant which used to reside in the premises of the king's palace. The Elephant was very dear to the king, so he was well-fed and well-treated. There was also a dog who lived near the elephant's shed. He was very weak and skinny. He was always fascinated by the smell of rich sweet rice being fed to the royal elephant.

5 One day, the dog could no longer resist the aroma of the rice and somehow managed to sneak into the elephant's shed. He liked the rice so much that he started going there daily to eat the rice. For days, the huge elephant did not notice the small dog as he was busy enjoying the delicious food. Gradually, the dog grew bigger and stronger eating such rich food. Finally, the elephant noticed him and allowed him access to the food.

10 The elephant enjoyed the company of the dog and started sharing his food with him. They also started spending time with each other and soon became good friends. They ate together, slept together, and played together. While playing, the elephant would hold the dog in his trunk and swing him back and forth. Soon neither of them was happy without the other. They became great friends and did not want to be separated from each other.

15 Then one day, a man saw the dog and asked the elephant-keeper, "I want to buy this dog. What price do you want for it? "The elephant-keeper didn't own the dog but sold it and extracted a sum of money from this deal. The man took the dog to his home village, which was far away. The king's elephant became very sad after this incident. He missed his friend a lot and started

neglecting everything. He did not want to do anything without his dear friend, so he stopped eating, drinking and even bathing.

Finally, the elephant-keeper reported this to the king; however, he did not mention anything about the dog. The king had a wise minister, who was known for his keen understanding of animals. The king ordered the minister, "Go to the elephant's shed and find out the reason for the elephant's condition". The intelligent minister went to the elephant's shed and found the elephant very sad. He examined the elephant and asked the elephant-keeper, "there is nothing wrong with this elephant's body, then why does he look so sad? I think this elephant is grief stricken, possibly due to the loss of a dear friend. Do you know if this elephant shared a close friendship with anyone?"

The elephant-keeper said, "There was a dog who used to eat, sleep and play with the elephant. He was taken by a stranger three days ago". The minister went back to the king and said, "Your majesty, in my opinion, the royal elephant is not sick, but he is lonesome without his dear friend, the dog". The king said, "You're right, friendship is one of the most wonderful things of life. Do you know where that dog is?"

The Minister replied, "elephant-keeper has informed me that a stranger took him away and he doesn't know his whereabouts". The king asked, "How can we bring back my elephant's friend and make him happy again?" The minister suggested, "Your Majesty, make a declaration, that whoever has the dog that used to live at the royal elephant's shed will be penalized". The king did the same and the man who had taken the dog, instantly turned him loose when he heard the proclamation.

As soon as he was freed, the dog ran back as fast as he could to the elephant's shed. The elephant was so delighted to see the dog that he picked his friend up with his trunk and swung him back and forth. The dog wagged his tail, while the elephant's sparkled with happiness. The king was content to see the elephant happy once again and rewarded the minister for his wise judgment.

① **What was the minister's diagnosis of the elephant's condition?**

- ☐ A- The elephant hated his keeper
- ☐ B- The elephant was lonely
- ☐ C- The elephant was starving
- ☐ D- The elephant had hurt his leg and was is pain

② **What method did the Minister suggest to the King to get back the dog?**

- ☐ A- To declare that whoever had that particular dog would be punished
- ☐ B- To keep a bowl of rice for the dog in the elephant's shed so that he he could be lured back to the place
- ☐ C- To command the elephant-keeper to look for the dog in the village
- ☐ D- To persuade the elephant to call out to the dog

③ **Why had the elephant become very sad?**

- ☐ A- He no longer got his daily bowl of rice
- ☐ B- He was unhappy with the king for having sold the dog
- ☐ C- He missed his friend, the dog
- ☐ D- He was sold to an unknown man by his keeper

④ **What did the elephant-keeper do to the dog?**

- ☐ A- He sold the dog to an unknown man for a price
- ☐ B- He hit the dog as the dog was eating the elephant's food
- ☐ C- He killed the dog
- ☐ D- He complained to the king about the dog

(5) Which of the following would be the most appropriate title for the passage?

☐ A- Friends and enemies

☐ B- The playful Dog

☐ C- The king and the minister

☐ D- The bond of friendship

(6) Why was the elephant taken care of?

☐ A- He was a very special elephant as he could talk to dogs

☐ B- He was a very loyal elephant

☐ C- The elephant was very dear to the king

☐ D- He was weak, and the king had a lot of sympathy for him

(7) Why did the dog start going to the elephant's shed everyday?

☐ A- He liked the elephant a lot and wanted to be friend with him

☐ B- He was being fed by the king everyday

☐ C- He was fond of the elephant's shed

☐ D- He liked the taste of the rice being fed to the elephant

(8) What did the dog do as soon as he was set free?

☐ A- He ate rice to his heart's content

☐ B- He thanked the king for his kindness.

☐ C- He ran away from the kingdom to a place far away

☐ D- He ran back to his friend, the elephant

⑨ **What of the following can definitely be said about the elephant-keeper?**

> **1. He was greedy.**
>
> **2. He was insensitive.**
>
> **3. He was brave.**

☐ **A-** Only 1

☐ **B-** Only 2

☐ **C-** Only 1 and 2

☐ **D-** Only 2 and 3

⑩ **Which of the following can definitely be said about the king?**

> **1. He was compassionate.**
>
> **2. He was deceitful.**
>
> **3. He loved animals.**

☐ **A-** Only 1

☐ **B-** Only 1 and 3

☐ **C-** Only 1 and 2

☐ **D-** Only 2

⑪ **Why did the stranger set the dog free?**

☐ **A-** He was concerned about the dog's well-being

☐ **B-** He was concerned about the elephant's loneliness

☐ **C-** He was scared

☐ **D-** None of the above

(12) Why was the minister rewarded by the king?

☐ A- He found the dog

☐ B- He cured the elephant

☐ C- He devised a plan to find the dog which worked

☐ D- He deceived the king into thinking that he deserve the reward

(13) How did the elephant feel after seeing the dog again?

☐ A- He was very happy

☐ B- He was neutral about it

☐ C- He was not happy to see him back

☐ D- He was angry to see him

(14) Choose the option that is most SIMILAR in meaning to the given word as used in the passage:

PREMISES (line 1)

☐ A- Area

☐ B- Land

☐ C- Boundary

☐ D- All of the above

(15) Choose the option that is most SIMILAR in meaning to the given word as used in the passage:

AROMA (line 5)

☐ A- Taste

☐ B- Beauty

☐ C- Smell

☐ D- Sight

(16) **Choose the option that is most SIMILAR in meaning to the given word as used in the passage:**

        SNEAK   **(line 5)**

☐   **A-** Peak

☐   **B-** Move

☐   **C-** Enter stealthily

☐   **D-** Run

(17) **Choose the option that is most SIMILAR in meaning to the given word as used in the passage:**

        EXTRACTED   **(line 16)**

☐   **A-** Pulled

☐   **B-** Inserted

☐   **C-** Receive

☐   **D-** Dug Out

(18) **Choose the option that is most SIMILAR in meaning to the given word as used in the passage:**

        DECLARATION   **(line 36)**

☐   **A-** Pact

☐   **B-** Praise

☐   **C-** Announcement

☐   **D-** Writ

⑲ Choose the option that is OPPOSITE in meaning to the given word as used in the passage:

RESIST (line 5)

☐ **A-** Give in

☐ **B-** Please

☐ **C-** Struggle

☐ **D-** Try out

⑳ Choose the option that is OPPOSITE in meaning to the given word as used in the passage:

CONTENT (line 43)

☐ **A-** Satisfied

☐ **B-** Pleased

☐ **C-** Happy

☐ **D-** Dissatisfied

SECTION 2: VERBAL REASONING – CLOZE

YOU HAVE 9 MINUTES TO COMPLETE THIS SECTION

THERE ARE 21 QUESTIONS IN THIS SECTION

(1) Long ago people knew very little about the **w** __ **r** **l** __.

(2) The **e** **a** __ __ __ was thought to be flat.

(3) Hence, if a person walked long enough in one **d** __ **r** __ __ **t** __ __ **n**,

(4) he would finally reach the **e** __ **g** __ of the world and fall off.

(5) Today we know that the earth is not a flat **r** **e** **c** __ **a** **n** **g** __ __ __ __

(6) block; it is **r** __ __ __ **d**.

(7) We owe this knowledge to the **e** __ **p** __ __ __ **e** **r** **s** who made long

(8) **v** __ __ **a** **g** __ __ to find new routes and discover new lands.

(9) They kept accurate records of the **o** __ **e** __ **n** __ they crossed and the

(10) strange lands they visited. From these records, they drew up a **m** __ __ of

(11) the world. In this way, they ended the belief of a **f** **l** __ __ world.

(12) Though we know the earth much better today, the **s** **p** **i** **r** __ __ of

(13) **e** __ **p** **l** **o** __ __ __ **i** **o** **n** has not, as a result, come to an end. The

(14) desire for **a** **d** **v** __ **n** __ __ __ __, the urge to set foot on a wild shore

⑮ and the **c** __ **r** __ __ **s** __ **t y** for far-flung places are still alive.

⑯ **B e** __ __ **d** __ __, not all places on earth have been fully

⑰ **e x p** __ __ __ __ __. Places like deserts,

⑱ **m o** __ n __ __ __ n __ , oceans, and polar regions still have secrets

⑲ and **m y s t** __ __ __ __ __ to amaze us. It is fortunate for us that there

⑳ are still many things to be **d** __ **s c** __ **v** __ __ __ __ which means

㉑ that the earth remains rich and **w** __ **n d** __ **r** __ __**l**.

SECTION 3: VERBAL REASONING – ODD ONE OUT

YOU HAVE 6 MINUTES TO COMPLETE THIS SECTION

THERE ARE 18 QUESTIONS IN THIS SECTION

Three of the words in each list are linked. Mark the word that is **not** related to these three.

①

Banana	Mango	Cashew	Guava
☐	☐	☐	☐

②

Car	Motorcycle	Jeep	Bicycle
☐	☐	☐	☐

③

Crab	Tortoise	Fish	Frog
☐	☐	☐	☐

④

Mix	Stir	Blend	Shake
☐	☐	☐	☐

⑤

Violet	Indigo	Blue	Pink
☐	☐	☐	☐

6	Brother	Sister	Niece	Daughter
	☐	☐	☐	☐

7	Tap	Bucket	Pitcher	Glass
	☐	☐	☐	☐

8	Hill	River	Dam	Mountain
	☐	☐	☐	☐

9	Equilateral	Scalene	Isosceles	Obtuse
	☐	☐	☐	☐

10	Square	Rhombus	Rectangle	Cube
	☐	☐	☐	☐

11	June	August	January	December
	☐	☐	☐	☐

12	Volleyball	Football	Tennis	Basketball
	☐	☐	☐	☐

⑬

Dog	Wolf	Cat	Fish
☐	☐	☐	☐

⑭

Grin	Shout	Cry	Yell
☐	☐	☐	☐

⑮

Appealing	Attractive	Alluring	Hideous
☐	☐	☐	☐

⑯

Centimetre	Millimetre	Inch	Kilometre
☐	☐	☐	☐

⑰

Clear	Blur	Obscure	Vague
☐	☐	☐	☐

⑱

Paragraph	Sentence	Line	Page
☐	☐	☐	☐

SECTION 4: VERBAL REASONING - ANTONYMS

YOU HAVE 6 MINUTES TO COMPLETE THIS SECTION

THERE ARE 18 QUESTIONS IN THIS SECTION

Choose the word which means the opposite, or nearly the opposite of the word given on the left.

1. **ENORMOUS**

soft	average	tiny	weak
☐	☐	☐	☐

2. **COMISSIONED**

started	finished	closed	terminated
☐	☐	☐	☐

3. **ARTIFICIAL**

natural	fake	solid	beautiful
☐	☐	☐	☐

4. **EXODUS**

leaving	influx	return	restoration
☐	☐	☐	☐

5. **RELINQUISH**

abdicate	renounce	deny	possess
☐	☐	☐	☐

⑥	**EXPAND**	convert ☐	condense ☐	congest ☐	conclude ☐
⑦	**MORTAL**	immortal ☐	divine ☐	eternal ☐	spiritual ☐
⑧	**OBEYING**	ordering ☐	following ☐	requesting ☐	scolding ☐
⑨	**FRAUDULENT**	candid ☐	genuine ☐	original ☐	fake ☐
⑩	**STARTLED**	amused ☐	relaxed ☐	endless ☐	astonished ☐
⑪	**FRESH**	faulty ☐	sluggish ☐	disgraceful ☐	stale ☐
⑫	**CULPABLE**	blameless ☐	defendable ☐	careless ☐	responsible ☐
⑬	**AWARE**	uncertain ☐	ignorant ☐	doubtful ☐	sure ☐

⑭ **SHRINK**

contract	stretch	spoil	expand
☐	☐	☐	☐

⑮ **COMMON**

rare	small	pretty	poor
☐	☐	☐	☐

⑯ **COMFORT**

uncomfort	miscomfort	discomfort	None of these
☐	☐	☐	☐

⑰ **EVASIVE**

free	elusive	liberal	frank
☐	☐	☐	☐

⑱ **GREGARIOUS**

antisocial	glorious	horrendous	similar
☐	☐	☐	☐

SECTION 5: NON-VERBAL REASONING

YOU HAVE 9 MINUTES TO COMPLETE THIS SECTION

THERE ARE 18 QUESTIONS IN THIS SECTION

SELECT THE SHAPE ON THE RIGHT WHICH IS A ROTATED FORM OF THE BIG SHAPE ON THE LEFT.

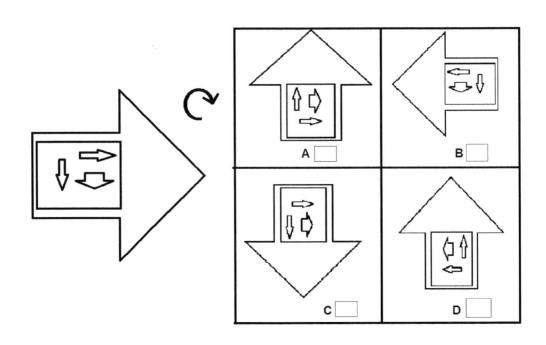

②

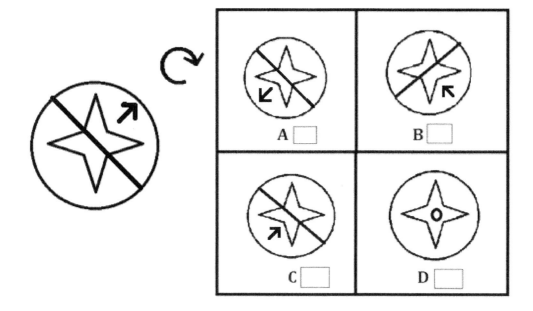

③

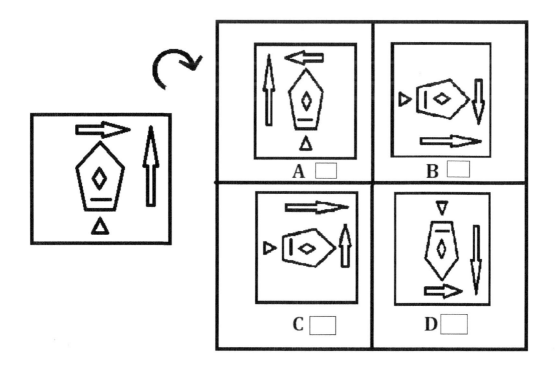

④

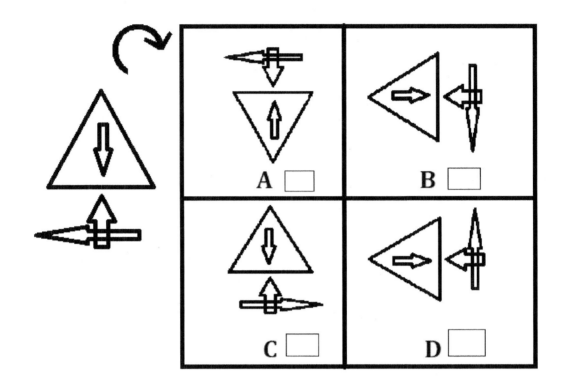

⑤

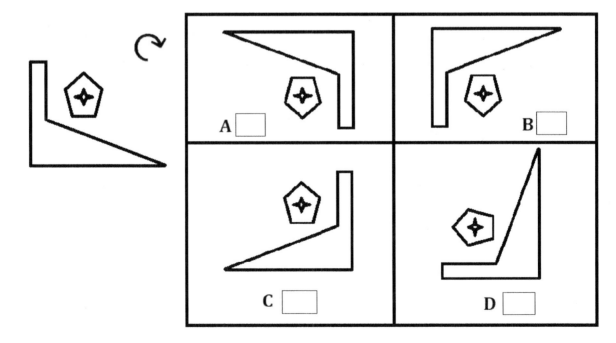

⑥

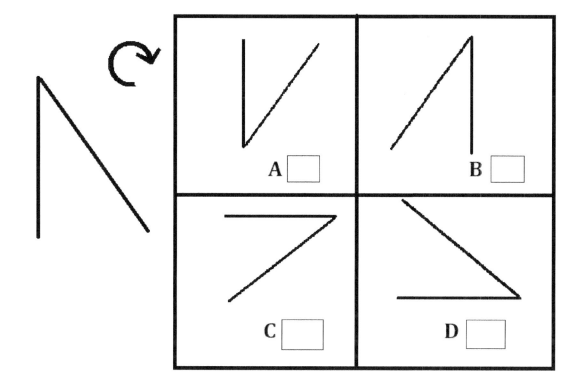

A ☐   B ☐

C ☐   D ☐

⑦

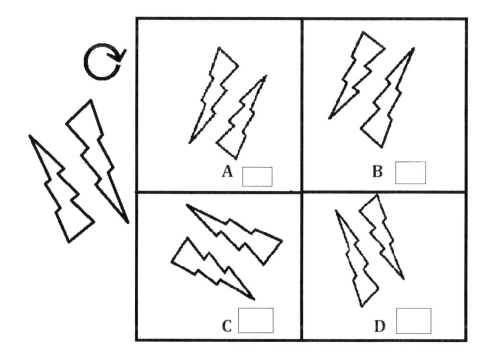

A ☐   B ☐

C ☐   D ☐

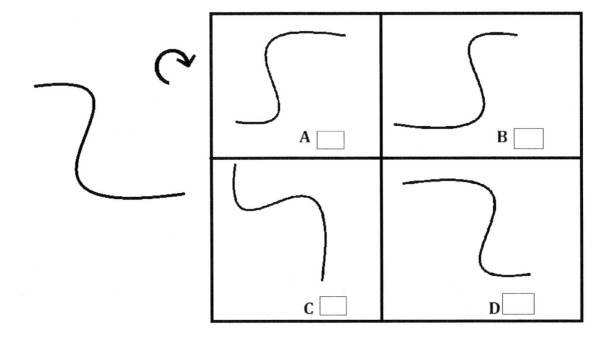

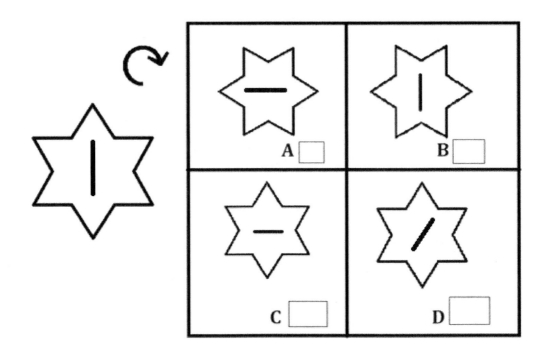

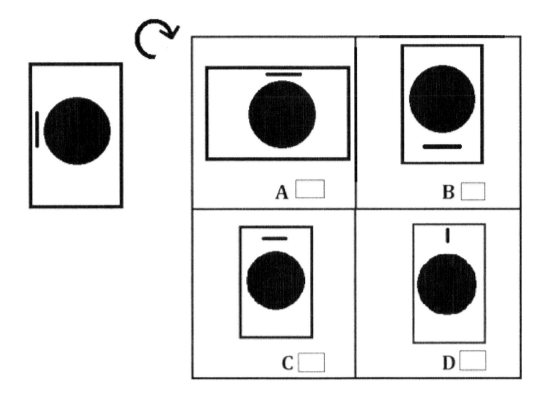

FIND THE SHAPE THAT SHOULD FILL THE EMPTY SQUARE ON THE LEFT

⑪

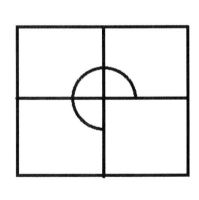

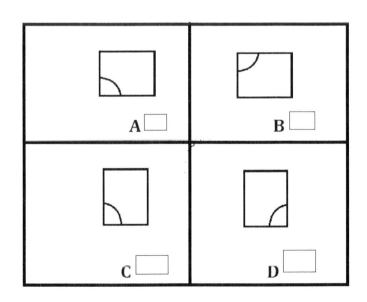

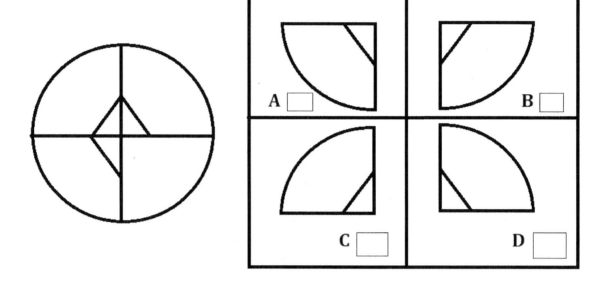

A ☐ B ☐ C ☐ D ☐

⑬

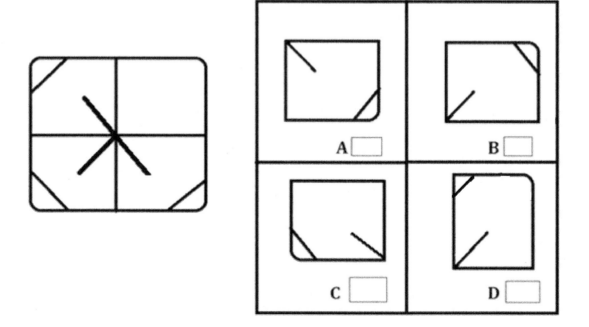

A ☐ B ☐ C ☐ D ☐

SELECT THE SHAPE THAT IS THE 2 Dimensional (2D) TOP-VIEW OF THE 3 Dimensional (3D) SHAPE ON THE LEFT

 14

A ☐

B ☐

C ☐

D ☐

 15

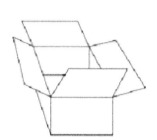

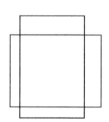

A ☐

B ☐

C ☐

D ☐

⑯

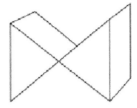

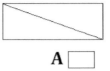

A ☐

B ☐

C ☐

D ☐

⑰

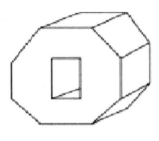

A ☐

B ☐

C ☐

D ☐

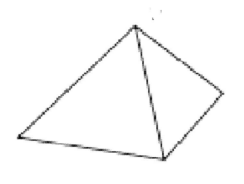

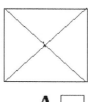

A ☐

B ☐

C ☐

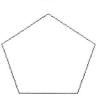

D ☐

<u>THE END</u>

SET B: PAPER 2

There are 3 Sections in this examination:

Section 1: Numerical Reasoning

Section 2: Verbal Reasoning – Cloze

Section 3: Non-Verbal Reasoning

<u>Note:</u> The exam has a total of 80 questions (including parts of multi-part questions)

SECTION 1: NUMERICAL REASONING

YOU HAVE 34 MINUTES TO COMPLETE THIS SECTION

THERE ARE 14 MULTI-PART QUESTIONS IN THIS SECTION

(1) Tommy and his friends went to his uncle's orchard at countryside to pick up fruits. They brought identical baskets with them for fruit picking. Each basket, when full, carried 15 apples, 15 oranges, or 20 guavas.

Tommy and his friends filled 24 baskets in total. 1/3rd of the baskets were filled with oranges, half of the baskets with guavas, and the rest with apples.

a) How many apples did Tommy and his friends pick in total?

□□

b) What is the total number of fruits that Tommy and his friends picked?

□□□

c) Express the ratio of the number of each fruit picked in following order:
Apples : Oranges : Guavas

□ : □ : □

The baskets are emptied, and all the fruits are put together on a heap.

d) What is the probability that a fruit picked at random from the heap is apple?
(Round up your answer to two decimal places)

□□ . □□ %

(2) Two complete normal packs of 52 playing cards are shuffled together and put on a table. Jimmy draws one card at random, and it turns out to be the Ace of Diamonds.

a) What is the probability that the second card drawn from those cards is an Ace?

$$\frac{3}{104} \qquad \frac{3}{103} \qquad \frac{4}{104} \qquad \frac{3}{51} \qquad \frac{7}{103}$$

☐ ☐ ☐ ☐ ☐

b) What is the probability that the second card drawn will be a Diamond Card?

$$\frac{25}{103} \qquad \frac{12}{104} \qquad \frac{12}{103} \qquad \frac{13}{51} \qquad \frac{13}{103}$$

☐ ☐ ☐ ☐ ☐

The Ace of Diamond drawn earlier is put back into the shuffled decks.

c) Find the probability of picking up a black card.

$$\frac{25}{52} \qquad \frac{13}{52} \qquad 1 \qquad \frac{51}{103} \qquad \frac{1}{2}$$

☐ ☐ ☐ ☐ ☐

d) Find the probability of picking up either an ace or a picture card.

$$\frac{4}{13} \qquad \frac{30}{104} \qquad \frac{13}{52} \qquad \frac{26}{52} \qquad \frac{4}{104}$$

☐ ☐ ☐ ☐ ☐

(3) Consider the rectangular box shown below.

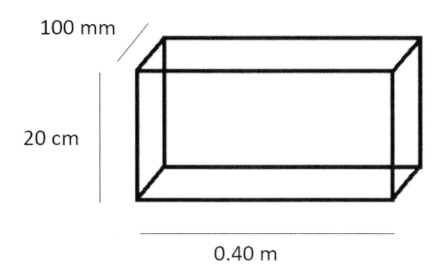

100 mm

20 cm

0.40 m

a) What is the volume of the box in mm³?

_____ mm³

b) Find the total surface are of the box (all six sides) in cm² ?

_____ cm²

c) What is the maximum amount of water, that the box can hold in litres? (1m³=1000 liters)

_____ litres

d) How many litres of water will the box hold if it is filled up to the height of 10cm out of total height of 20cm?

_____ litres

4 The diagram below shows the rectangle ABCD. E is the midpoint of DC.

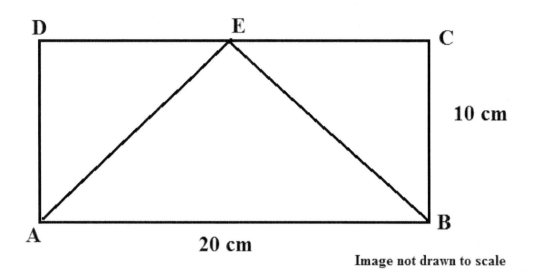

Image not drawn to scale

a) What is the difference in areas of Δ AED and Δ BEC?

_____ cm²

b) What is the area of Δ AEB?

_____ cm²

c) Find the perimeter and area of the rectangle

Area: _____ cm²   Perimeter:_____cm

d) Find the measure of ∠AEB

_____ °

5 A bookshop sells a certain brand of notebooks. The price is as follows:

£1.50 for 50 pages notebook

£2.00 for 75 pages notebook

£2.50 for 100 pages notebook

The complete cost (material, printing etc.) of one notebook is as follows:

£0.50 + (£0.01 x number of pages)

Profit = Selling price – Cost Price

a) What is the profit per notebook for 50 pages notebook?

£ _____

b) How much more profit per notebook does the bookshop earn when selling a 100 pages notebook as compared to selling the 75 pages notebook?

£ _____

c) On a particular day, the book shop sold fifteen 50-pages notebooks, ten 75-pages notebooks, and eight 100-pages notebooks. What is the total profit earned?

£ _____

d) What would be the selling price of 50-pages notebook if the profit needs to be equal to the 100-pages notebook?

£ _____

(6) The graph shows the one hour cycling journey by Danny.

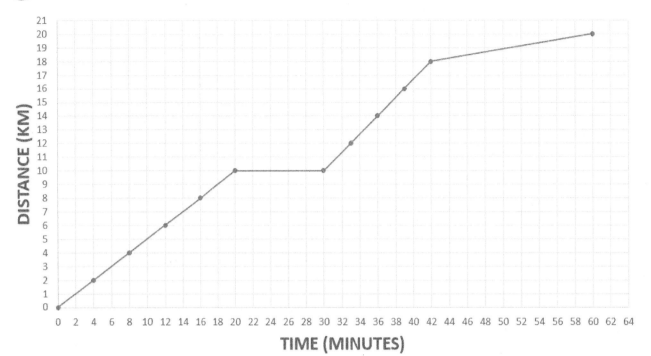

a) What is the total distance covered by Danny?

_____Km

b) What is Danny doing between 20-30 minutes?

Accelerating	Decelerating	Resting	Constant speed
☐	☐	☐	☐

c) At which interval is Danny's speed the fastest?

0-20 minutes	20-30 minutes	30-42 minutes	42-60 minutes
☐	☐	☐	☐

d) At which interval is Danny's speed the lowest?

0-20 minutes	0-60 minutes	30-42 minutes	42-60 minutes
☐	☐	☐	☐

7 A businessman divides £10 million of his wealth amongst his loyal employees as follows:

Employee Name	Amount
Laura	20%
Tom	1/10
Sara	2/5
John	0.5 million
Michael	?

a) What is the amount of money that Michael will receive?

£ _____ millions

b) Which person gets the highest amount of money?

Laura	Tom	Sara	John	Michael
☐	☐	☐	☐	☐

c) What percentage of the wealth is received by John?

_____ %

£2 million is later added to the dedicated wealth for loyal employees. Thus, the total amount becomes £12 million. This is distributed in the same percentage as the original amount.

d) How much extra amount would John receive from the added £2 million?

£ _____

8 The temperature of boiled water is noted at 1-minute intervals and is shown in the table below

Time (Minutes)	Temperature (°C)
0	100
1	94
2	88
3	82
4	76
5	70

a) What is the temperature of the water after 6 minutes?

70°C	68°C	66°C	64°C	62°C
☐	☐	☐	☐	☐

b) Which expression describes the temperature after 'n' minutes?

100n	100n – n	100n - 6n	100n + 6n	100 – 6n
☐	☐	☐	☐	☐

c) Assuming the temperature drops at the same rate, how long would it take the water's temperature to fall below 30°C?

11 minutes	12 minutes	13 minutes	14 minutes	15 minutes
☐	☐	☐	☐	☐

9 The diagram below shows a rectangle ACEG, and various triangles, as marked.

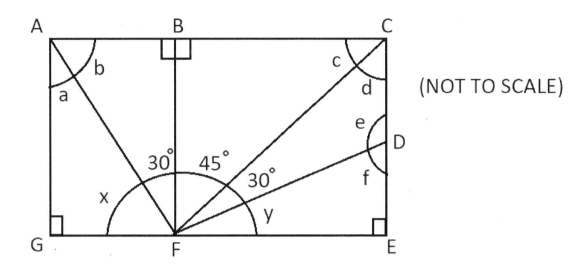

(NOT TO SCALE)

a) What is the size of the angle marked 'a'?

_____°

b) What is the size of the angle marked 'd'?

_____°

c) What is the size of the angle marked 'f'?

_____°

d) What is the size of the angle marked 'y'?

_____°

10 A man was 25 years old when his daughter was born. He is now twice as old as his daughter.

a) What is the present age of the daughter?

_____ years

b) How long from now would it take for the daughter to be 2/3rd of her father's age?

_____ years

11 A classroom has a total of 40 pupils. 1/5th of the pupils are girls. Half of the girls are less than 5 feet tall. The boys are all more than 5 feet tall.

a) How many girls are there in the class?

_____

b) How many pupils in the class are more than 5 feet tall?

_____

(12) A survey was taken from a group of people about what they have for breakfast. The results are shown in the table below:

BREAKFAST	Number of people
Fried Eggs	● ● ◖
Omelet	● ◗
Cereals	◖ ◖
Boiled Eggs	◖
Tea	◗ ◗

● = 8 people

a) How many people eat Fried Eggs in their breakfast?

_____

b) How many people eat Omelet in their breakfast?

_____

c) How many more people eat Cereals than those who eat boiled eggs in their breakfast?

_____

It is assumed that all the people who recorded their responses only eat one of the 5 items mentioned in the table above.

d) How many people in total recorded their responses for the survey?

_____

(13) A rectangular field is twice as long as it is wide. The total area of the land is 128 ft².

a) What is the length of the field in feet?

_____ ft

b) What is the width of the field in feet?

_____ ft

It is given that the field is covered with boundary wall on the three sides. The uncovered side is the shorter side.

c) What is the length of the boundary wall in feet?

_____ ft

(14) Simon and Sarah go to an ice-cream parlor. The price of the ice-cream depends upon the size of the ice-cream as well as the toppings. The following information is given:

SIZE	PRICE
Small	£2.5
Medium	£3.2
Large	£3.8
Extra Large	£4.0

BASIC TOPPINGS (£0.25 per topping)	SPECIAL TOPPINGS (£0.50 per topping)
Chocolate Chips, Sprinkles, Nuts, Caramel, Whipped Cream	Mixed Fruits, Chocolate Flakes, Fudge, Blueberries

a) Simon buys extra-large ice-cream with sprinkles, nuts, and blueberries. How much does it cost him?

£_____

b) Sarah buys a medium cup ice-cream with flakes and whipped cream. How much does it cost her?

£_____

c) What can be the maximum cost of an ice-cream cup which includes all the toppings available?

£_____

On Fridays, there is a special discount of 20% off on all sizes of ice-cream, 40% off on basic toppings, and 50% off on special toppings.

d) Sarah buys a small size ice-cream with whipped cream and mixed fruits. How much does this cost her?

£_____

SECTION 2: VERBAL REASONING - CLOZE

YOU HAVE 5 MINUTES TO COMPLETE THIS SECTION

THERE ARE 14 QUESTIONS IN THIS SECTION

(1)
- ☐ Unlike
- ☐ Despite
- ☐ Dislike
- ☐ Like

The honeybee is a very unusual kind of insect. _____ other insects which live

(2)
- ☐ alone
- ☐ together
- ☐ separately
- ☐ privately

alone, the honeybee lives as a member of a community. These bees live _____

in what is known as a bee colony. The head of the colony is called the queen bee.

(3)
- ☐ many
- ☐ most
- ☐ final
- ☐ rest

(4)
- ☐ at
- ☐ to
- ☐ in
- ☐ of

She is larger than the _____ of the bees. Her main task _____

the colony is to lay eggs. Most of the other bees are the worker bees. These bees

(5).
- ☐ collect
- ☐ take
- ☐ eat
- ☐ put

_____ nectar and pollen from the flowers. The nectar that is carried by

(6)
- ☐ towards
- ☐ into
- ☐ by
- ☐ for

the worker bees is deposited in the hive and then converted _____ honey.

(7) The worker bees also help look
☐ to
☐ for
☐ towards
☐ after
the young bees.

(8) As soon as the eggs are
☐ hatch
☐ hatched
☐ hatches
☐ broken
, the worker bees feed the young bees

(9)
☐ in
☐ to
☐ by
☐ with
pollen and nectar. The third type of bee found in the colony is the

(10) drone or male bee. The main task of
☐ such
☐ this
☐ that
☐ male
a bee is to enable the queen bee to lay

(11) eggs. The queen bee has a life
☐ period
☐ time
☐ span
☐ length
of approximately three years. During this

(12) period, she would have
☐ laid
☐ given
☐ taken
☐ born
more than half a million eggs.

(13)
☐ When
☐ After
☐ By
☐ During
the queenbee is dying, a new queen would be groomed.

This new queen would eventually take over the 'duties' of the old queen when the

(14)
☐ former
☐ latter
☐ later
☐ previous
dies.

SECTION 3: NON - VERBAL REASONING

YOU HAVE 6 MINUTES TO COMPLETE THIS SECTION

THERE ARE 16 QUESTIONS IN THIS SECTION

SELECT THE SHAPE THAT IS THE 2D TOP-VIEW OF THE 3D SHAPE ON THE LEFT

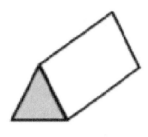
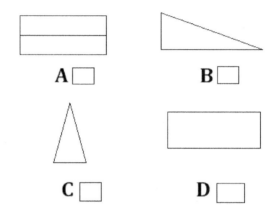

A   B

C   D

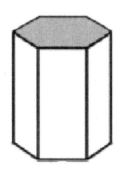
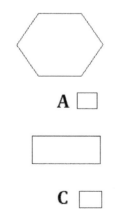
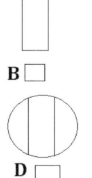

A   B

C   D

③

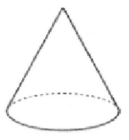

A ☐

B ☐

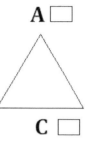

C ☐

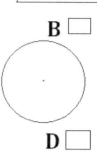

D ☐

④

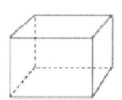

A ☐

B ☐

C ☐

D ☐

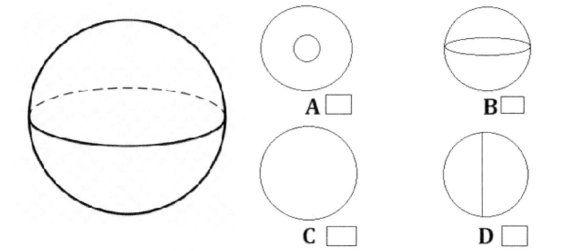

A □
B □
C □
D □

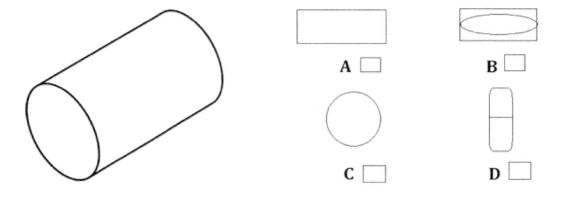

A □
B □
C □
D □

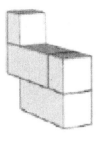

A ☐   B ☐

C ☐   D ☐

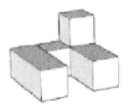

A ☐   B ☐

C ☐   D ☐

⑨

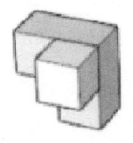

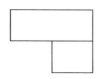

A ☐

B ☐

C ☐

D ☐

⑩

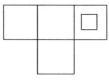

A ☐

B ☐

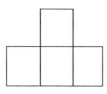

C ☐

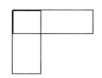

D ☐

SELECT THE FIGURE ON THE RIGHT WHICH IS A ROTATED FORM OF THE BIG FIGURE ON THE LEFT.

⑪

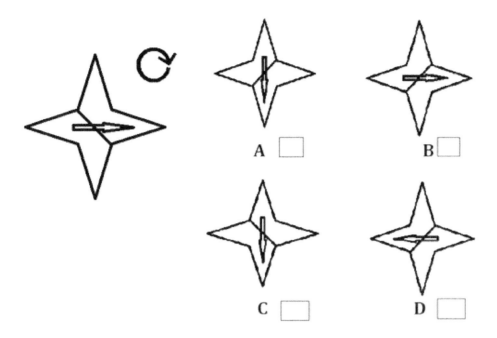

A ☐   B ☐

C ☐   D ☐

⑫

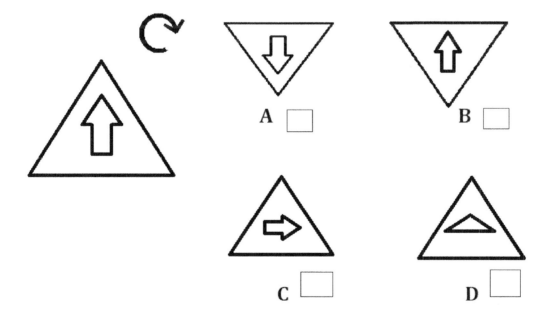

A ☐   B ☐

C ☐   D ☐

⑬

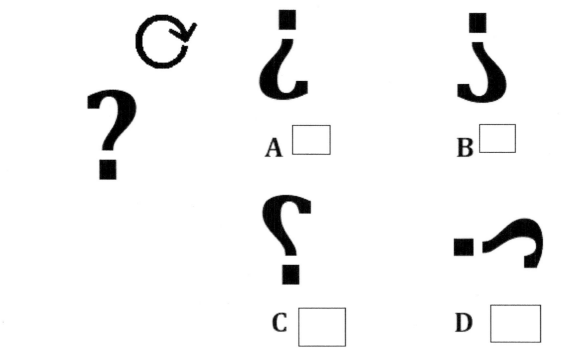

A ☐

B ☐

C ☐

D ☐

⑭

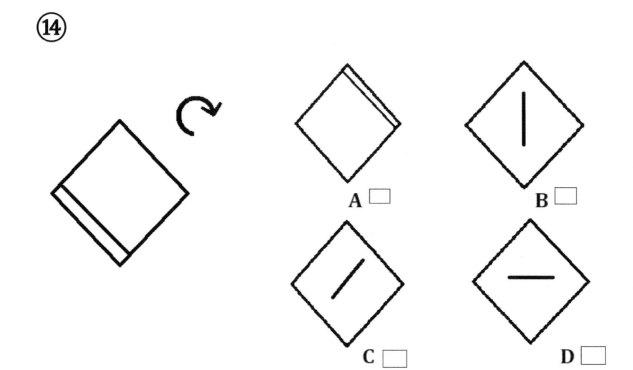

A ☐

B ☐

C ☐

D ☐

⑮

A ☐

B ☐

C ☐

D ☐

⑯

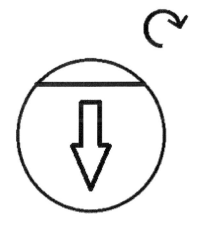

A ☐

B ☐

C ☐

D ☐

THE END

Answer Sheets

SECTION 1

Pupil's Name:

Test Date:

EXAMPLE

father	☐
mother	☐
brother	▬
sister	☐

1

at	☐
to	☐
in	☐
of	☐

2

collect	☐
take	☐
eat	☐
put	☐

3

soon	☐
early	☐
late	☐
not	☐

4

should	☐
would	☐
shall	☐
could	☐

5

unlike	☐
despite	☐
dislike	☐
like	☐

6

should	☐
would	☐
may	☐
can	☐

7

should	☐
would	☐
may	☐
can	☐

8

them	☐
their	☐
there	☐
these	☐

9

them	☐
their	☐
there	☐
these	☐

10

in	☐
to	☐
by	☐
with	☐

11

should	☐
would	☐
may	☐
can	☐

12

towards	☐
into	☐
by	☐
for	☐

13

them	☐
their	☐
there	☐
these	☐

14

than	☐
then	☐
from	☐
by	☐

15

at	☐
to	☐
in	☐
of	☐

16

its	☐
it's	☐
to	☐
it is	☐

SECTION 2

① a

[0]	[0]	[0]	
[1]	[1]	[1]	
[2]	[2]	[2]	
[3]	[3]	[3]	
[4]	[4]	[4]	
[5]	[5]	[5]	
[6]	[6]	[6]	
[7]	[7]	[7]	
[8]	[8]	[8]	
[9]	[9]	[9]	

① b

		%
[0]	[0]	
[1]	[1]	
[2]	[2]	
[3]	[3]	
[4]	[4]	
[5]	[5]	
[6]	[6]	
[7]	[7]	
[8]	[8]	
[9]	[9]	

① c

[0]	[0]	[0]	
[1]	[1]	[1]	
[2]	[2]	[2]	
[3]	[3]	[3]	
[4]	[4]	[4]	
[5]	[5]	[5]	
[6]	[6]	[6]	
[7]	[7]	[7]	
[8]	[8]	[8]	
[9]	[9]	[9]	

① d

[0]	[0]	[0]	
[1]	[1]	[1]	
[2]	[2]	[2]	
[3]	[3]	[3]	
[4]	[4]	[4]	
[5]	[5]	[5]	
[6]	[6]	[6]	
[7]	[7]	[7]	
[8]	[8]	[8]	
[9]	[9]	[9]	

① e

		%
[0]	[0]	
[1]	[1]	
[2]	[2]	
[3]	[3]	
[4]	[4]	
[5]	[5]	
[6]	[6]	
[7]	[7]	
[8]	[8]	
[9]	[9]	

② a

1/4	☐
1/2	☐
2/3	☐
1/3	☐
1	☐

② b

1/2	☐
1/4	☐
1/6	☐
1/8	☐
1	☐

② c

1/9	☐
1/8	☐
1	☐
1/3	☐
3/5	☐

② d

1/9	☐
1/8	☐
1	☐
1/3	☐
3/5	☐

③ a

			m²
[0]	[0]	[0]	
[1]	[1]	[1]	
[2]	[2]	[2]	
[3]	[3]	[3]	
[4]	[4]	[4]	
[5]	[5]	[5]	
[6]	[6]	[6]	
[7]	[7]	[7]	
[8]	[8]	[8]	
[9]	[9]	[9]	

③ b

			m²
[0]	[0]	[0]	
[1]	[1]	[1]	
[2]	[2]	[2]	
[3]	[3]	[3]	
[4]	[4]	[4]	
[5]	[5]	[5]	
[6]	[6]	[6]	
[7]	[7]	[7]	
[8]	[8]	[8]	
[9]	[9]	[9]	

③ c

			m³
[0]	[0]	[0]	
[1]	[1]	[1]	
[2]	[2]	[2]	
[3]	[3]	[3]	
[4]	[4]	[4]	
[5]	[5]	[5]	
[6]	[6]	[6]	
[7]	[7]	[7]	
[8]	[8]	[8]	
[9]	[9]	[9]	

③ d

			m
[0]	[0]	[0]	
[1]	[1]	[1]	
[2]	[2]	[2]	
[3]	[3]	[3]	
[4]	[4]	[4]	
[5]	[5]	[5]	
[6]	[6]	[6]	
[7]	[7]	[7]	
[8]	[8]	[8]	
[9]	[9]	[9]	

④ a

100	☐
0	☐
1200	☐
500	☐
400	☐

④ b

200m to the south	☐
200m to the east	☐
0 m	☐
100m to the north	☐

④ c

300m to the south	☐
300m to the north	☐
At his original position	☐
100m to the west	☐

⑤ a

£		.		
	[0]		[0]	[0]
	[1]		[1]	[1]
	[2]		[2]	[2]
	[3]		[3]	[3]
	[4]		[4]	[4]
	[5]		[5]	[5]
	[6]		[6]	[6]
	[7]		[7]	[7]
	[8]		[8]	[8]
	[9]		[9]	[9]

⑤ b

£		.		
	[0]		[0]	[0]
	[1]		[1]	[1]
	[2]		[2]	[2]
	[3]		[3]	[3]
	[4]		[4]	[4]
	[5]		[5]	[5]
	[6]		[6]	[6]
	[7]		[7]	[7]
	[8]		[8]	[8]
	[9]		[9]	[9]

⑤ c

£		.		
	[0]		[0]	[0]
	[1]		[1]	[1]
	[2]		[2]	[2]
	[3]		[3]	[3]
	[4]		[4]	[4]
	[5]		[5]	[5]
	[6]		[6]	[6]
	[7]		[7]	[7]
	[8]		[8]	[8]
	[9]		[9]	[9]

⑤ d

£		.		
	[0]		[0]	[0]
	[1]		[1]	[1]
	[2]		[2]	[2]
	[3]		[3]	[3]
	[4]		[4]	[4]
	[5]		[5]	[5]
	[6]		[6]	[6]
	[7]		[7]	[7]
	[8]		[8]	[8]
	[9]		[9]	[9]

⑤ e

£			.		
	[0]	[0]		[0]	[0]
	[1]	[1]		[1]	[1]
	[2]	[2]		[2]	[2]
	[3]	[3]		[3]	[3]
	[4]	[4]		[4]	[4]
	[5]	[5]		[5]	[5]
	[6]	[6]		[6]	[6]
	[7]	[7]		[7]	[7]
	[8]	[8]		[8]	[8]
	[9]	[9]		[9]	[9]

⑥ a

(14,16)	
(-4, -6)	
(15, 5)	
(-5,15)	
(-5,-15)	

⑥ b

(20, 5)	
(5, 20)	
(5, -20)	
(-20, 5)	
(-20,-5)	

⑥ c

Tom's Place	
Sara's place	
At a random point	
At origin	
Harry's place	

⑥ d

Adam - Sara	
Adam - Harry	
Adam - Mary	
Adam - Michael	

⑥ e

Tom - Sara	
Tom - Michael	
Harry - Mary	
Adam – Anna	

⑦ a

[0]	[0]	[0]
[1]	[1]	[1]
[2]	[2]	[2]
[3]	[3]	[3]
[4]	[4]	[4]
[5]	[5]	[5]
[6]	[6]	[6]
[7]	[7]	[7]
[8]	[8]	[8]
[9]	[9]	[9]

⑦ b

[0]	[0]	[0]
[1]	[1]	[1]
[2]	[2]	[2]
[3]	[3]	[3]
[4]	[4]	[4]
[5]	[5]	[5]
[6]	[6]	[6]
[7]	[7]	[7]
[8]	[8]	[8]
[9]	[9]	[9]

⑦ c

		%
[0]	[0]	
[1]	[1]	
[2]	[2]	
[3]	[3]	
[4]	[4]	
[5]	[5]	
[6]	[6]	
[7]	[7]	
[8]	[8]	
[9]	[9]	

⑦ d

[0]	[0]	[0]
[1]	[1]	[1]
[2]	[2]	[2]
[3]	[3]	[3]
[4]	[4]	[4]
[5]	[5]	[5]
[6]	[6]	[6]
[7]	[7]	[7]
[8]	[8]	[8]
[9]	[9]	[9]

Section 2 continued..

⑧ a			⑧ b	
[0]	[0]		[0]	[0]
[1]	[1]		[1]	[1]
[2]	[2]		[2]	[2]
[3]	[3]		[3]	[3]
[4]	[4]		[4]	[4]
[5]	[5]		[5]	[5]
[6]	[6]		[6]	[6]
[7]	[7]		[7]	[7]
[8]	[8]		[8]	[8]
[9]	[9]		[9]	[9]

⑨a	
360 degrees	
180 degrees	
90 degrees	
45 degrees	

⑨b	
360 degrees	
180 degrees	
90 degrees	
45 degrees	

⑨c	
11: 00	
12: 00	
11: 30	
12: 20	

⑨d	
11: 00	
12: 00	
11: 30	
12: 20	

SECTION 3

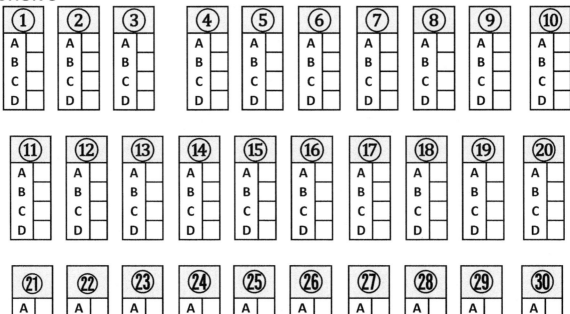

SECTION 1

Pupil's Name:

Test Date:

①	②	③		④	⑤	⑥	⑦	⑧	⑨	⑩
A	A	A		A	A	A	A	A	A	A
B	B	B		B	B	B	B	B	B	B
C	C	C		C	C	C	C	C	C	C
D	D	D		D	D	D	D	D	D	D

⑪	⑫	⑬	⑭	⑮	⑯
A	A	A	A	A	A
B	B	B	B	B	B
C	C	C	C	C	C
D	D	D	D	D	D

SECTION 2

①	②	③		④	⑤	⑥	⑦	⑧	⑨	⑩
A	A	A		A	A	A	A	A	A	A
B	B	B		B	B	B	B	B	B	B
C	C	C		C	C	C	C	C	C	C
D	D	D		D	D	D	D	D	D	D

SECTION 3

① 1
plane	
even	
flat	
mansion	

② 2
scale	
reach	
trivia	
range	

③ 3
vicious	
plot	
mean	
propose	

④ 4
mallet	
nail	
smack	
pound	

⑤ 5
light	
flimsy	
downy	
clever	

⑥ 6
iris	
pupil	
university	
class	

⑦ 7
communication	
Note	
Moral	
Spot	

⑧ 8
bear	
stand	
lug	
ear	

⑨ 9
grumble	
noun	
object	
fight	

⑩ 10
hunger	
speedy	
waterfall	
fast	

⑪ 11
force	
might	
possibly	
April	

⑫ 12
just	
fair	
only	
beautiful	

SECTION 4

①

u	n		m	p						t
		e[ ]			i[ ]	t[ ]	r[ ]	e[ ]	n[ ]	
		i[ ]			o[ ]	r[ ]	s[ ]	a[ ]	m[ ]	
		o[ ]			k[ ]	s[ ]	t[ ]	o[ ]	x[ ]	

②

u	g		
		e[ ]	i[ ]
		l[ ]	y[ ]
		o[ ]	k[ ]

③

a	n		i			
		e[ ]		i[ ]	m[ ]	r[ ]
		d[ ]		e[ ]	t[ ]	s[ ]
		c[ ]		u[ ]	n[ ]	t[ ]

④

u	n		t		
		e[ ]		i[ ]	d[ ]
		i[ ]		e[ ]	s[ ]
		u[ ]		u[ ]	n[ ]

⑤

	n									y
i[ ]		e[ ]	o[ ]	t[ ]	i[ ]	o[ ]	r[ ]	e[ ]	b[ ]	
r[ ]		f[ ]	l[ ]	r[ ]	o[ ]	u[ ]	s[ ]	a[ ]	s[ ]	
e[ ]		o[ ]	e[ ]	s[ ]	k[ ]	a[ ]	t[ ]	i[ ]	t[ ]	

⑥

a	r				i	c			
		t[ ]	i[ ]	c[ ]			u[ ]	o[ ]	l[ ]
		u[ ]	o[ ]	d[ ]			i[ ]	u[ ]	n[ ]
		v[ ]	a[ ]	f[ ]			o[ ]	a[ ]	s[ ]

⑦

l		n		e	n	
	e[ ]		i[ ]			o[ ]
	l[ ]		e[ ]			s[ ]
	a[ ]		u[ ]			t[ ]

⑧

s	e		i	o		
		s[ ]			o[ ]	o[ ]
		t[ ]			s[ ]	s[ ]
		r[ ]			u[ ]	t[ ]

SECTION 4

⑨

f		x		
	e[ ]		i[ ]	d[ ]
	o[ ]		e[ ]	s[ ]
	i[ ]		u[ ]	n[ ]

⑩

a		q			t
	c[ ]		i[ ]	i[ ]	
	d[ ]		e[ ]	e[ ]	
	e[ ]		u[ ]	u[ ]	

⑪

a	l				
		v[ ]	a[ ]	a[ ]	a[ ]
		w[ ]	y[ ]	y[ ]	y[ ]
		x[ ]	s[ ]	s[ ]	s[ ]

⑫

t	h		o	r		t			l
		e[ ]			e[ ]	e[ ]	a[ ]	a[ ]	
		i[ ]			i[ ]	i[ ]	b[ ]	b[ ]	
		o[ ]			o[ ]	o[ ]	c[ ]	c[ ]	

⑬

	a		h	e			
a[ ]		a[ ]			l[ ]	r[ ]	l[ ]
b[ ]		b[ ]			o[ ]	o[ ]	o[ ]
c[ ]		c[ ]			r[ ]	l[ ]	r[ ]

⑭

a	m		t			
		a[ ]		i[ ]	i[ ]	r[ ]
		e[ ]		e[ ]	e[ ]	s[ ]
		u[ ]		u[ ]	u[ ]	t[ ]

⑮

	s		e		
	w[ ]		i[ ]	r[ ]	
	v[ ]		e[ ]	s[ ]	
	u[ ]		u[ ]	t[ ]	

⑯

	u		
a[ ]		j[ ]	l[ ]
b[ ]		k[ ]	n[ ]
d[ ]		l[ ]	o[ ]

SECTION 5

①	
wrong	
enormous	
week	
eroded	

②	
start	
release	
length	
grasp	

③	
natural	
synthetic	
solid	
beautiful	

④	
truth	
story	
return	
restoration	

⑤	
tranquil	
renounce	
deny	
possess	

⑥	
convert	
condense	
congest	
swell	

⑦	
immortal	
divine	
perishable	
spiritual	

⑧	
invest	
inaugurate	
relinquish	
prepare	

⑨	
candid	
genuine	
original	
swindling	

⑩	
finished	
relax	
endless	
astonished	

⑪	
faulty	
sluggish	
disgraceful	
new	

⑫	
pretty	
ugly	
weak	
responsible	

⑬	
uncertain	
ignorant	
doubtful	
sure	

⑭	
contract	
stretch	
spoil	
expand	

⑮	
rare	
small	
petty	
usual	

⑯	
uncomfort	
miscomfort	
discomfort	
none of these	

⑰	
free	
honest	
liberal	
ambiguous	

⑱	
unfriendly	
glorious	
horrendous	
social	

SECTION 6

1

			%
[0]	[0]	[0]	
[1]	[1]	[1]	
[2]	[2]	[2]	
[3]	[3]	[3]	
[4]	[4]	[4]	
[5]	[5]	[5]	
[6]	[6]	[6]	
[7]	[7]	[7]	
[8]	[8]	[8]	
[9]	[9]	[9]	

2

		%
[0]	[0]	
[1]	[1]	
[2]	[2]	
[3]	[3]	
[4]	[4]	
[5]	[5]	
[6]	[6]	
[7]	[7]	
[8]	[8]	
[9]	[9]	

3

£			.		
	[0]	[0]		[0]	[0]
	[1]	[1]		[1]	[1]
	[2]	[2]		[2]	[2]
	[3]	[3]		[3]	[3]
	[4]	[4]		[4]	[4]
	[5]	[5]		[5]	[5]
	[6]	[6]		[6]	[6]
	[7]	[7]		[7]	[7]
	[8]	[8]		[8]	[8]
	[9]	[9]		[9]	[9]

4

	.		Km/hr
[0]		[0]	
[1]		[1]	
[2]		[2]	
[3]		[3]	
[4]		[4]	
[5]		[5]	
[6]		[6]	
[7]		[7]	
[8]		[8]	
[9]		[9]	

5

		Km
[0]	[0]	
[1]	[1]	
[2]	[2]	
[3]	[3]	
[4]	[4]	
[5]	[5]	
[6]	[6]	
[7]	[7]	
[8]	[8]	
[9]	[9]	

6

		Km/hr
[0]	[0]	
[1]	[1]	
[2]	[2]	
[3]	[3]	
[4]	[4]	
[5]	[5]	
[6]	[6]	
[7]	[7]	
[8]	[8]	
[9]	[9]	

7

		.			Km/hr
[0]	[0]		[0]	[0]	
[1]	[1]		[1]	[1]	
[2]	[2]		[2]	[2]	
[3]	[3]		[3]	[3]	
[4]	[4]		[4]	[4]	
[5]	[5]		[5]	[5]	
[6]	[6]		[6]	[6]	
[7]	[7]		[7]	[7]	
[8]	[8]		[8]	[8]	
[9]	[9]		[9]	[9]	

8

[0]	[0]
[1]	[1]
[2]	[2]
[3]	[3]
[4]	[4]
[5]	[5]
[6]	[6]
[7]	[7]
[8]	[8]
[9]	[9]

9

	/	
[0]		[0]
[1]		[1]
[2]		[2]
[3]		[3]
[4]		[4]
[5]		[5]
[6]		[6]
[7]		[7]
[8]		[8]
[9]		[9]

10

[0]	[0]	[0]	[0]
[1]	[1]	[1]	[1]
[2]	[2]	[2]	[2]
[3]	[3]	[3]	[3]
[4]	[4]	[4]	[4]
[5]	[5]	[5]	[5]
[6]	[6]	[6]	[6]
[7]	[7]	[7]	[7]
[8]	[8]	[8]	[8]
[9]	[9]	[9]	[9]

11

Monday	
Tuesday	
Thursday	
Friday	

SECTION 6

⑫			
			ft²
[0]	[0]	[0]	
[1]	[1]	[1]	
[2]	[2]	[2]	
[3]	[3]	[3]	
[4]	[4]	[4]	
[5]	[5]	[5]	
[6]	[6]	[6]	
[7]	[7]	[7]	
[8]	[8]	[8]	
[9]	[9]	[9]	

⑬	
19	
20	
21	
22	

⑭					
		.			m²
[0]	[0]		[0]	[0]	
[1]	[1]		[1]	[1]	
[2]	[2]		[2]	[2]	
[3]	[3]		[3]	[3]	
[4]	[4]		[4]	[4]	
[5]	[5]		[5]	[5]	
[6]	[6]		[6]	[6]	
[7]	[7]		[7]	[7]	
[8]	[8]		[8]	[8]	
[9]	[9]		[9]	[9]	

⑮	
6m	
5 m	
1.25m	
2.5m	

⑯	
[0]	[0]
[1]	[1]
[2]	[2]
[3]	[3]
[4]	[4]
[5]	[5]
[6]	[6]
[7]	[7]
[8]	[8]
[9]	[9]

⑰		
		m²
[0]	[0]	
[1]	[1]	
[2]	[2]	
[3]	[3]	
[4]	[4]	
[5]	[5]	
[6]	[6]	
[7]	[7]	
[8]	[8]	
[9]	[9]	

⑱	
64	
48	
128	
44	

⑳	
1 day	
5 days	
Half day	
2 days	

⑲	
30	
50	
25	
15	

㉑	
5%	
10%	
20%	
50%	

㉒	
30	
34	
36	
49	

㉓	
15	
13	
14	
17	

SECTION 1

Pupil's Name:

Test Date:

	1	2	3	4	5	6	7	8	9	10
A										
B										
C										
D										

	11	12	13	14	15	16	17	18	19	20
A										
B										
C										
D										

SECTION 2

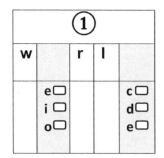

1

w		r	l
e ☐			c ☐
i ☐			d ☐
o ☐			e ☐

2

e	a			
		s ☐	s ☐	g ☐
		r ☐	r ☐	h ☐
		t ☐	t ☐	s ☐

3

d		r		t		n
	i ☐		i ☐	a ☐	i ☐	i ☐
	e ☐		e ☐	b ☐	e ☐	e ☐
	u ☐		u ☐	c ☐	o ☐	o ☐

④

e		g	
	a☐		i☐
	b☐		e☐
	d☐		u☐

⑤

r	e	c		a	n	g				
			r☐				o☐	e☐	a☐	r☐
			s☐				a☐	a☐	o☐	s☐
			t☐				u☐	l☐	u☐	t☐

⑥

r			d
	i☐	u☐	o☐
	o☐	i☐	u☐
	a☐	o☐	n☐

⑦

e		p					e	r	s
	z☐		l☐	o☐	r☐	o☐			
	y☐		m☐	s☐	s☐	i☐			
	x☐		n☐	t☐	t☐	e☐			

⑧

v			a	g	
	e☐	e☐		e☐	o☐
	y☐	y☐		y☐	s☐
	o☐	o☐		o☐	t☐

⑨

o			a		
	c☐	e☐		e☐	o☐
	y☐	y☐		n☐	s☐
	o☐	o☐		o☐	t☐

⑩

m		
	e☐	p☐
	o☐	s☐
	a☐	n☐

⑪

f	l	
	a☐	a☐
	y☐	t☐
	s☐	s☐

⑫

s	p	i	r		
				t□ q□	
				i□ r□	
				s□ t□	

⑬

e		p	l	o				i	o	n
	x□				r□ a□ s□					
	y□				o□ o□ t□					
	z□				l□ e□ u□					

⑭

a	d	v		n					
			i□		r□	i□	r□	o□	
			e□		s□	e□	s□	f□	
			u□		t□	u□	t□	e□	

⑮

c		r			s		t	y
	i□		o□	i□		o□		
	e□		e□	o□		i□		
	u□		i□	u□		e□		

⑯

B	e			d		
		s□ i□			i□ r□	
		t□ o□			o□ s□	
		u□ a□			e□ t□	

⑰

e	x	p					
			t□	a□	r□	e□	a□
			n□	e□	s□	f□	d□
			l□	o□	t□	g□	e□

⑱

m	o		n			n	
		i□		r□	i□	i□	r□
		e□		s□	e□	e□	s□
		u□		t□	a□	a□	t□

⑲

m	y	s	t					
				u□	q□	a□	o□	s□
				i□	r□	u□	f□	t□
				e□	s□	i□	e□	r□

20

d		s	c		v				
	a☐ o☐ i☐			r☐ o☐ l☐		a☐ o☐ e☐	s☐ t☐ r☐	e☐ o☐ u☐	a☐ b☐ d☐

21

w		n	d		r			l
	u☐ a☐ o☐			u☐ e☐ o☐		g☐ f☐ h☐	u☐ e☐ o☐	

SECTION 3

① 1
Banana	
Mango	
Cashew	
Guava	

② 2
Car	
Motorcycle	
Jeep	
Cycle	

③ 3
Crab	
Tortoise	
Fish	
Frog	

④ 4
Mix	
Stir	
Blend	
Shake	

⑤ 5
Violet	
Indigo	
Blue	
Pink	

⑥ 6
Brother	
Sister	
Niece	
Daughter	

⑦ 7
Tap	
Bucket	
Pitcher	
Glass	

⑧ 8
Hill	
River	
Dam	
Mountain	

⑨ 9
Equilateral	
Scalene	
Isosceles	
Obtuse	

⑩ 10
Square	
Circle	
Rectangle	
Cube	

⑪ 11
June	
August	
January	
December	

⑫ 12
Volleyball	
Football	
Tennis	
Basketball	

⑬ 13
Dog	
Wolf	
Cat	
Fish	

⑭ 14
Grin	
Shout	
Cry	
Yell	

⑮ 15
Appealing	
Attractive	
Alluring	
Hideous	

⑯ 16
Centimetre	
Millimetre	
Inch	
Kilometre	

⑰ 17
Clear	
Blur	
Obscure	
Vague	

⑱ 18
Paragraph	
Sentence	
Line	
Page	

SECTION 4

① 1
soft	
average	
tiny	
weak	

② 2
Started	
finished	
closed	
terminated	

③ 3
natural	
fake	
solid	
beautiful	

④ 4
leaving	
influx	
return	
restoration	

⑤ 5
abdicate	
renounce	
deny	
possess	

⑥ 6
convert	
condense	
congest	
conclude	

⑦ 7
immortal	
divine	
eternal	
spiritual	

⑧ 8
ordering	
following	
requesting	
scolding	

⑨ 9
candid	
genuine	
original	
fake	

⑩ 10
amused	
relaxed	
endless	
astonished	

⑪ 11
faulty	
sluggish	
disgraceful	
stale	

⑫ 12
blameless	
defendable	
careless	
responsible	

⑬ 13
uncertain	
ignorant	
doubtful	
sure	

⑭ 14
contract	
stretch	
spoil	
expand	

⑮ 15
rare	
small	
pretty	
poor	

⑯ 16
uncomfort	
miscomfort	
discomfort	
none of these	

⑰ 17
free	
honest	
liberal	
frank	

⑱ 18
antisocial	
glorious	
horrendous	
similar	

SECTION 5

① 1 A B C D
② 2 A B C D
③ 3 A B C D
④ 4 A B C D
⑤ 5 A B C D
⑥ 6 A B C D
⑦ 7 A B C D
⑧ 8 A B C D
⑨ 9 A B C D
⑩ 10 A B C D

⑪ 11 A B C D
⑫ 12 A B C D
⑬ 13 A B C D
⑭ 14 A B C D
⑮ 15 A B C D
⑯ 16 A B C D
⑰ 17 A B C D
⑱ 18 A B C D

SECTION 1

Pupil's Name:

Test Date:

① a	
[0]	[0]
[1]	[1]
[2]	[2]
[3]	[3]
[4]	[4]
[5]	[5]
[6]	[6]
[7]	[7]
[8]	[8]
[9]	[9]

① b		
[0]	[0]	[0]
[1]	[1]	[1]
[2]	[2]	[2]
[3]	[3]	[3]
[4]	[4]	[4]
[5]	[5]	[5]
[6]	[6]	[6]
[7]	[7]	[7]
[8]	[8]	[8]
[9]	[9]	[9]

① c		:		:	
[0]		[0]		[0]	
[1]		[1]		[1]	
[2]		[2]		[2]	
[3]		[3]		[3]	
[4]		[4]		[4]	
[5]		[5]		[5]	
[6]		[6]		[6]	
[7]		[7]		[7]	
[8]		[8]		[8]	
[9]		[9]		[9]	

① d		.			%
[0]	[0]		[0]	[0]	
[1]	[1]		[1]	[1]	
[2]	[2]		[2]	[2]	
[3]	[3]		[3]	[3]	
[4]	[4]		[4]	[4]	
[5]	[5]		[5]	[5]	
[6]	[6]		[6]	[6]	
[7]	[7]		[7]	[7]	
[8]	[8]		[8]	[8]	
[9]	[9]		[9]	[9]	

② a	
3/104	
3/103	
4/104	
3/51	
7/103	

② b	
25/103	
12/104	
12/103	
13/51	
13/103	

② c	
25/52	
13/52	
1	
51/103	
1/2	

② d	
4/13	
30/104	
13/52	
26/52	
4/104	

Section 1

③ a

									mm³
[0]	[0]	[0]	[0]	[0]	[0]	[0]	[0]	[0]	
[1]	[1]	[1]	[1]	[1]	[1]	[1]	[1]	[1]	
[2]	[2]	[2]	[2]	[2]	[2]	[2]	[2]	[2]	
[3]	[3]	[3]	[3]	[3]	[3]	[3]	[3]	[3]	
[4]	[4]	[4]	[4]	[4]	[4]	[4]	[4]	[4]	
[5]	[5]	[5]	[5]	[5]	[5]	[5]	[5]	[5]	
[6]	[6]	[6]	[6]	[6]	[6]	[6]	[6]	[6]	
[7]	[7]	[7]	[7]	[7]	[7]	[7]	[7]	[7]	
[8]	[8]	[8]	[8]	[8]	[8]	[8]	[8]	[8]	
[9]	[9]	[9]	[9]	[9]	[9]	[9]	[9]	[9]	

③ b

					cm²
[0]	[0]	[0]	[0]	[0]	
[1]	[1]	[1]	[1]	[1]	
[2]	[2]	[2]	[2]	[2]	
[3]	[3]	[3]	[3]	[3]	
[4]	[4]	[4]	[4]	[4]	
[5]	[5]	[5]	[5]	[5]	
[6]	[6]	[6]	[6]	[6]	
[7]	[7]	[7]	[7]	[7]	
[8]	[8]	[8]	[8]	[8]	
[9]	[9]	[9]	[9]	[9]	

③ c

			.			litres
[0]	[0]	[0]		[0]	[0]	
[1]	[1]	[1]		[1]	[1]	
[2]	[2]	[2]		[2]	[2]	
[3]	[3]	[3]		[3]	[3]	
[4]	[4]	[4]		[4]	[4]	
[5]	[5]	[5]		[5]	[5]	
[6]	[6]	[6]		[6]	[6]	
[7]	[7]	[7]		[7]	[7]	
[8]	[8]	[8]		[8]	[8]	
[9]	[9]	[9]		[9]	[9]	

③ d

		.		litres
[0]	[0]		[0]	[0]
[1]	[1]		[1]	[1]
[2]	[2]		[2]	[2]
[3]	[3]		[3]	[3]
[4]	[4]		[4]	[4]
[5]	[5]		[5]	[5]
[6]	[6]		[6]	[6]
[7]	[7]		[7]	[7]
[8]	[8]		[8]	[8]
[9]	[9]		[9]	[9]

④ a

			.			cm²
[0]	[0]	[0]		[0]	[0]	
[1]	[1]	[1]		[1]	[1]	
[2]	[2]	[2]		[2]	[2]	
[3]	[3]	[3]		[3]	[3]	
[4]	[4]	[4]		[4]	[4]	
[5]	[5]	[5]		[5]	[5]	
[6]	[6]	[6]		[6]	[6]	
[7]	[7]	[7]		[7]	[7]	
[8]	[8]	[8]		[8]	[8]	
[9]	[9]	[9]		[9]	[9]	

④ b

			cm²
[0]	[0]	[0]	
[1]	[1]	[1]	
[2]	[2]	[2]	
[3]	[3]	[3]	
[4]	[4]	[4]	
[5]	[5]	[5]	
[6]	[6]	[6]	
[7]	[7]	[7]	
[8]	[8]	[8]	
[9]	[9]	[9]	

④ c

			cm²
[0]	[0]	[0]	
[1]	[1]	[1]	
[2]	[2]	[2]	
[3]	[3]	[3]	
[4]	[4]	[4]	
[5]	[5]	[5]	
[6]	[6]	[6]	
[7]	[7]	[7]	
[8]	[8]	[8]	
[9]	[9]	[9]	

④ c

		cm
[0]	[0]	
[1]	[1]	
[2]	[2]	
[3]	[3]	
[4]	[4]	
[5]	[5]	
[6]	[6]	
[7]	[7]	
[8]	[8]	
[9]	[9]	

④ d

		.			°
[0]	[0]		[0]	[0]	[0]
[1]	[1]		[1]	[1]	[1]
[2]	[2]		[2]	[2]	[2]
[3]	[3]		[3]	[3]	[3]
[4]	[4]		[4]	[4]	[4]
[5]	[5]		[5]	[5]	[5]
[6]	[6]		[6]	[6]	[6]
[7]	[7]		[7]	[7]	[7]
[8]	[8]		[8]	[8]	[8]
[9]	[9]		[9]	[9]	[9]

⑤ a

£		.		
	[0]		[0]	[0]
	[1]		[1]	[1]
	[2]		[2]	[2]
	[3]		[3]	[3]
	[4]		[4]	[4]
	[5]		[5]	[5]
	[6]		[6]	[6]
	[7]		[7]	[7]
	[8]		[8]	[8]
	[9]		[9]	[9]

⑤ b

£		.		
	[0]		[0]	[0]
	[1]		[1]	[1]
	[2]		[2]	[2]
	[3]		[3]	[3]
	[4]		[4]	[4]
	[5]		[5]	[5]
	[6]		[6]	[6]
	[7]		[7]	[7]
	[8]		[8]	[8]
	[9]		[9]	[9]

⑤ c

£		.		
	[0]	[0]		[0]	[0]
	[1]	[1]		[1]	[1]
	[2]	[2]		[2]	[2]
	[3]	[3]		[3]	[3]
	[4]	[4]		[4]	[4]
	[5]	[5]		[5]	[5]
	[6]	[6]		[6]	[6]
	[7]	[7]		[7]	[7]
	[8]	[8]		[8]	[8]
	[9]	[9]		[9]	[9]

⑤ d

£		.		
	[0]		[0]	[0]
	[1]		[1]	[1]
	[2]		[2]	[2]
	[3]		[3]	[3]
	[4]		[4]	[4]
	[5]		[5]	[5]
	[6]		[6]	[6]
	[7]		[7]	[7]
	[8]		[8]	[8]
	[9]		[9]	[9]

⑥ a

		Km
[0]	[0]	
[1]	[1]	
[2]	[2]	
[3]	[3]	
[4]	[4]	
[5]	[5]	
[6]	[6]	
[7]	[7]	
[8]	[8]	
[9]	[9]	

⑥ b

Accelerating	
Decelerating	
Resting	
Constant Speed	

⑥ c

0-20 minutes	
20-30 minutes	
30-42 minutes	
42-60 minutes	

⑥ d

0-20 minutes	
0-60 minutes	
30-42 minutes	
42-60 minutes	

⑦ a

	.		millions
[0]		[0]	
[1]		[1]	
[2]		[2]	
[3]		[3]	
[4]		[4]	
[5]		[5]	
[6]		[6]	
[7]		[7]	
[8]		[8]	
[9]		[9]	

⑦ b

Laura	
Tom	
Sara	
John	
Michael	

⑦ c

	%
[0]	
[1]	
[2]	
[3]	
[4]	
[5]	
[6]	
[7]	
[8]	
[9]	

⑦ d

£						
	[0]	[0]	[0]	[0]	[0]	[0]
	[1]	[1]	[1]	[1]	[1]	[1]
	[2]	[2]	[2]	[2]	[2]	[2]
	[3]	[3]	[3]	[3]	[3]	[3]
	[4]	[4]	[4]	[4]	[4]	[4]
	[5]	[5]	[5]	[5]	[5]	[5]
	[6]	[6]	[6]	[6]	[6]	[6]
	[7]	[7]	[7]	[7]	[7]	[7]
	[8]	[8]	[8]	[8]	[8]	[8]
	[9]	[9]	[9]	[9]	[9]	[9]

⑧ a

70°C	
68°C	
66°C	
64°C	
62°C	

⑧ b

100n	
100n − n	
100n − 6n	
100n + 6n	
100 − 6n	

⑧ c

11 minutes	
12 minutes	
13 minutes	
14 minutes	
15 minutes	

⑨ a

		°
[0]	[0]	
[1]	[1]	
[2]	[2]	
[3]	[3]	
[4]	[4]	
[5]	[5]	
[6]	[6]	
[7]	[7]	
[8]	[8]	
[9]	[9]	

⑨ b

		°
[0]	[0]	
[1]	[1]	
[2]	[2]	
[3]	[3]	
[4]	[4]	
[5]	[5]	
[6]	[6]	
[7]	[7]	
[8]	[8]	
[9]	[9]	

⑨ c

		°
[0]	[0]	
[1]	[1]	
[2]	[2]	
[3]	[3]	
[4]	[4]	
[5]	[5]	
[6]	[6]	
[7]	[7]	
[8]	[8]	
[9]	[9]	

⑨ d

		°
[0]	[0]	
[1]	[1]	
[2]	[2]	
[3]	[3]	
[4]	[4]	
[5]	[5]	
[6]	[6]	
[7]	[7]	
[8]	[8]	
[9]	[9]	

⑩ a

		years
[0]	[0]	
[1]	[1]	
[2]	[2]	
[3]	[3]	
[4]	[4]	
[5]	[5]	
[6]	[6]	
[7]	[7]	
[8]	[8]	
[9]	[9]	

⑩ b

		years
[0]	[0]	
[1]	[1]	
[2]	[2]	
[3]	[3]	
[4]	[4]	
[5]	[5]	
[6]	[6]	
[7]	[7]	
[8]	[8]	
[9]	[9]	

⑪ a

[0]	[0]
[1]	[1]
[2]	[2]
[3]	[3]
[4]	[4]
[5]	[5]
[6]	[6]
[7]	[7]
[8]	[8]
[9]	[9]

⑪ b

[0]	[0]
[1]	[1]
[2]	[2]
[3]	[3]
[4]	[4]
[5]	[5]
[6]	[6]
[7]	[7]
[8]	[8]
[9]	[9]

⑫ a

[0]	[0]
[1]	[1]
[2]	[2]
[3]	[3]
[4]	[4]
[5]	[5]
[6]	[6]
[7]	[7]
[8]	[8]
[9]	[9]

⑫ b

[0]	[0]
[1]	[1]
[2]	[2]
[3]	[3]
[4]	[4]
[5]	[5]
[6]	[6]
[7]	[7]
[8]	[8]
[9]	[9]

⑫ c

[0]	[0]
[1]	[1]
[2]	[2]
[3]	[3]
[4]	[4]
[5]	[5]
[6]	[6]
[7]	[7]
[8]	[8]
[9]	[9]

⑫ d

[0]	[0]
[1]	[1]
[2]	[2]
[3]	[3]
[4]	[4]
[5]	[5]
[6]	[6]
[7]	[7]
[8]	[8]
[9]	[9]

⑬ a

		feet
[0]	[0]	
[1]	[1]	
[2]	[2]	
[3]	[3]	
[4]	[4]	
[5]	[5]	
[6]	[6]	
[7]	[7]	
[8]	[8]	
[9]	[9]	

⑬ b

		feet
[0]	[0]	
[1]	[1]	
[2]	[2]	
[3]	[3]	
[4]	[4]	
[5]	[5]	
[6]	[6]	
[7]	[7]	
[8]	[8]	
[9]	[9]	

⑬ c

		feet
[0]	[0]	
[1]	[1]	
[2]	[2]	
[3]	[3]	
[4]	[4]	
[5]	[5]	
[6]	[6]	
[7]	[7]	
[8]	[8]	
[9]	[9]	

⑭ a

£		.		
	[0]		[0]	[0]
	[1]		[1]	[1]
	[2]		[2]	[2]
	[3]		[3]	[3]
	[4]		[4]	[4]
	[5]		[5]	[5]
	[6]		[6]	[6]
	[7]		[7]	[7]
	[8]		[8]	[8]
	[9]		[9]	[9]

⑭ b

£		.		
	[0]		[0]	[0]
	[1]		[1]	[1]
	[2]		[2]	[2]
	[3]		[3]	[3]
	[4]		[4]	[4]
	[5]		[5]	[5]
	[6]		[6]	[6]
	[7]		[7]	[7]
	[8]		[8]	[8]
	[9]		[9]	[9]

⑭ c

£		.		
	[0]		[0]	[0]
	[1]		[1]	[1]
	[2]		[2]	[2]
	[3]		[3]	[3]
	[4]		[4]	[4]
	[5]		[5]	[5]
	[6]		[6]	[6]
	[7]		[7]	[7]
	[8]		[8]	[8]
	[9]		[9]	[9]

⑭ d

£		.		
	[0]		[0]	[0]
	[1]		[1]	[1]
	[2]		[2]	[2]
	[3]		[3]	[3]
	[4]		[4]	[4]
	[5]		[5]	[5]
	[6]		[6]	[6]
	[7]		[7]	[7]
	[8]		[8]	[8]
	[9]		[9]	[9]

SECTION 2

①	
Unlike	
Despite	
Dislike	
Like	

②	
Alone	
Together	
Separately	
Privately	

③	
Many	
Most	
Final	
Rest	

④	
At	
To	
In	
Of	

⑤	
Collect	
Take	
Eat	
Put	

⑥	
Towards	
Into	
By	
For	

⑦	
To	
For	
Towards	
After	

⑧	
Hatch	
Hatched	
Hatches	
Broken	

⑨	
In	
To	
By	
With	

⑩	
Such	
This	
That	
Male	

⑪	
Period	
Time	
Span	
Length	

⑫	
Laid	
Given	
Taken	
Born	

⑬	
When	
After	
By	
During	

⑭	
Former	
Latter	
Later	
Previous	

SECTION 3

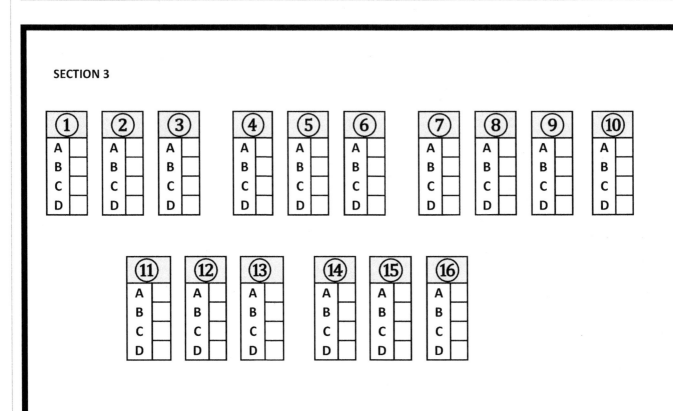

①		②		③		④		⑤		⑥		⑦		⑧		⑨		⑩	
A		A		A		A		A		A		A		A		A		A	
B		B		B		B		B		B		B		B		B		B	
C		C		C		C		C		C		C		C		C		C	
D		D		D		D		D		D		D		D		D		D	

⑪		⑫		⑬		⑭		⑮		⑯	
A		A		A		A		A		A	
B		B		B		B		B		B	
C		C		C		C		C		C	
D		D		D		D		D		D	

Answers
with
Explanations

Answer Sheet with Explanation
Exam A1
A1: Section 1 – Verbal Reasoning – Cloze:

1- Of

Many animals in the wild are suspicious and fearful of human beings.

2- Take

Many animals would take flight instantly when a human approaches.

3- Soon

Man, however, soon discovered

4- Could

That some animals could be tamed or domesticated.

5- Unlike

Unlike animals in the wild

6- Would

These animals would allow man to come close to them

7- Would

They would even allow their owners to stroke or pet them.

8- Their

They would even allow their owners to stroke or pet them.

9- Them

They would even allow their owners to stroke or pet them.

10- In

In olden times, man would domesticate animals by setting traps to catch their young.

11- Would

In early times, man would domesticate animals by setting traps to catch their young.

12- By

In early times, man would domesticate animals by setting traps to catch their young.

13- Their

In early times, man would domesticate animals by setting traps to catch their young.

14- Than

A young animal is far more easily domesticated than an adult one.

15- To

From young age, the animal learns to trust and obey its owner

16- Its

From young age, the animal learns to trust and obey its owner.

A1: Section 2 – Numerical Reasoning:

1 a) 375

(75/100)*500 = 375

1 b)   2%

(10/500)*100 = 2%

1 c) 5

(1/100)*500 = 5

1 d)   110

500 – 375 – 10 – 5 = 110

1 e) 22%

(110/500)*100 = 22%

2a) $\dfrac{1}{4}$

½ x ½ = $\dfrac{1}{4}$

2b) $\dfrac{1}{2}$

Probability of getting Heads on the first coin and Tails on the second coin = ½ x ½ = $\dfrac{1}{4}$

Probability of getting Heads on the second coin and Tails on the first coin = ½ x ½ = $\dfrac{1}{4}$

Hence Total Probability = ¼ + ¼ = 1/2

2c) $\dfrac{1}{8}$ ½ x½ x ½ = $\dfrac{1}{8}$

2d) $\dfrac{1}{8}$ ½ x½ x ½ = $\dfrac{1}{8}$

3a) 82 m^2

(10 x 7) + (2 x 6) = 82 m^2

3b) 518 m^2

(15 x 40) – 82 = 518 m^2

3c) 82 m^3

82 m^2 x 1m = 82 m^3

3d) 133 m

15 + 40 + 15 + 40 + 10 + 7 + 4 + 2 = 133m

4a) 0 m

After moving in the said directions, the person reached back to his original position, hence 0 m is the right answer.

4b) 200 m to the South

Apply the given conditions on the map given in the question, and we find that the person is 200m to the South from his original position.

4c) 300 m to the North.

5a) £0.25

£2.50 / 10 = £0.25 per pen.

5b) £0.40

£2.00 /5 = £0.40 per pen.

5c) £7.50

10 x £0.75 = £7.50

5d) £4.50

£2.00 for 5 pens

£2.50 for 10 pens

Total for 15 pens = £2.00 + £2.50 = £4.50

5e) £15.00

20 * £0.75= £15.00

6a) (-5, 15)

6b) (-20, 5)

6c) Tom's place

6d) Adam-Mary

Adam and Mary are farthest with 66 units in between them

6e) Harry-Mary

Harry and Mary are closest with only 8 units between them

7a) 125

(45/360) * 1000 = 125

7b) 125

(45/360) * 1000 = 125

7c) 25%

(90/360) *100 = 25%

7d) 500

(50/100) * 1000 = 500

8a) 60 years

Let son's age = s

Then, father's age = 3s

Also, 3s +20 = 2 x (s +20)

Solving for s: s = (2 x 20) - 20 = 60

8b) 20 years

Let son's age = s

Then, father's age = 3s

Also, 3s+20 = 2 x (s +20)

Solving for s: s = 20

9a) 90°

The minute-needle is at right angles to the original position after 15 minutes, hence 90 degrees.

9b) 360°

The hour-needle comes back to its original position after 12 hours; hence 360 degrees is the right answer.

9c) 11:00

720 degrees means two full cycles of minute needle, which means 2 hours. Hence the time will be 9:00 + 2:00 = 11:00

9d) 12:00

The hour-needle, when moving 90 degrees, would be moving 3 hours, hence the time will be 9:00 + 3:00 = 12:00

A1: Section 3 – Non - Verbal Reasoning:

1- C

We need to find the arrow which points away from the center to complete the pattern. Both C and D fulfill this, however, only C touches the correct border of the square, hence correct option is C.

2- C

C is the correct answer as the shape previously behind is now at front. The shading of the two shapes have changed as well.

3- D

D is the right answer. The main figure changes from grey to white. The outside shapes remain in the same positions however the color changes. Black becomes grey and grey becomes black. Following this pattern, only shape D fulfills the criteria.

4- A

The shading of the central shape and outer shape swap in each figure, hence only A is the possible answer

5- A

'A' is the correct answer as it completes the pattern

6- D

D is the right answer. The triangle is mirrored vertically and the colour of the circles swap.

7- D

'D' is the right answer. The white arrow becomes black.

8- B

B is correct. The second figure rotates 180 degrees, and the colour of circles is swapped, and the line becomes dotted. So, B is the correct option in this case.

9- C

C is correct because the arrow points towards center of the circle as should be the pattern. A and B also follow this, however, only C has correct colour and position of the rectangles.

10- A

A is the correct answer. The arrow must point to the centre, which makes A and C the only possible answers. However, pattern C is already present in the figure, whereas the pattern is being changed each time, hence A is the only possible correct answer.

11- A

A is the correct answer. The shape needs to be rotated 90 degrees without changing anything else, and only A follows this pattern, hence the correct answer.

12- D

Shape D since it is the only shape having no reflection symmetry.

13- B

Shape B since it is the only shape not having dotted element.

14- A

Shape A. Since the orientation of the 3-quartered circle is different.

15- D

Shape D. Because only shape D has 5-sided polygon whereas all other shapes have 4 sided.

16- D

Shape D because all other shapes have arrows before the box, whereas shape D has arrow after the box.

17- A

Shape A because only shape A has no reflection symmetry

18- D

Shape D because only shape D has whole column of same color.

19- C

Only shape C has no reflection symmetry.

20- A

Shape A, because only shape A has same outer and inner shapes, whereas all other figures have different outer and inner shapes.

21- C

Shape C. As this shape has vertical space filled with grey in all the triangles.

22- B

Shape B because it has both elements having solid lines of same colour without any hollow space.

23- A

Shape A is the correct representation of the top-view of the 3d shape

24- C

Shape C is the correct representation of the top-view of the 3d shape

25- B

Shape B is the correct representation of the top-view of the 3d shape

26- B

Shape B is the correct representation of the top-view of the 3d shape

27- A

Shape A is the correct representation of the top-view of the 3d shape

28- B

Shape B is the correct representation of the top-view of the 3d shape

29- B

Shape B is the correct representation of the top-view of the 3d shape

30- A

Shape A is the correct representation of the top-view of the 3d shape

Exam A2

A2: Section 1 – Verbal Reasoning – Comprehension 1:

1-   D

The passage is all about thrill and fright, hence option 'D' is the correct answer.

2-   A

Jagged and Irregular are closest in meaning

3-   A

"Keen Interest" since Sherlock was eager to know where the sound was coming from

4-   A

'Alert and curious' best describes Sherlock's condition in the passage

5-   D

Physical and mental strength

6-   A

Yell, moan and cry are the only set of words in which all words are related to sound.

7-   C
Struggling while chasing the sound.

8-   D

How the detective chased the sound

9-   A

his death was the result of extreme violence.

10- C

Thrill

11- A

Swiftly means quickly

12- D

Hound means a hunting dog

13- B

Shouted loudly

14- C

Last paragraph. Refer to the last sentence "The moan had been the passing of his soul"

15- C

Hark means listen

16- A

An acrobatic act

6

A2: Section 2 – Verbal Reasoning – Comprehension 2:

1- C

Highlight the dramatic effect of changing scenes

2- A

Emotions at witnessing nature's might

3- D

Orchestrate here means demonstrate

4- D

He was holding onto the ship tightly

5- C

Build anticipation of the coming storm

6- B

A shiver of cold went through me

7- B

Uncontrolled rush of water

8- A

Impact and severity of his feelings

9- C

Line 23: The water did not look to be eighty feet away. The ship was sinking.

10- B

Unable to move due to shoc

A2: Section 3 – Verbal Reasoning – Multiple Meanings

1- Flat	2- Range	7- Note	8- Bear
3- Mean	4- Pound	9- Object	10- Fast
5- Light	6- Pupil	11- Might	12- Fair

A2: Section 4 – Verbal Reasoning – Antonyms:

1- Unimportant	2- Ugly	9- Fixed	10- Acquit
3- Ancient	4- United	11- Always	12- Theoretical
5- Inferiority	6- Artificial	13- Bachelor	14- Amateur
7- Lenient	8- Serious	15- Sweet	16- Dull

A2: Section 5 – Verbal Reasoning – Synonyms:

1- Wrong

2- Grasp

3- Synthetic

4- Story

5- Tranquil

6- Swell

7- Perishable

8- Inaugurate

9- Swindling

10- Astonished

11- New

12- Pretty

13- Sure

14- Contract

15- Usual

16- None of these

17- Ambiguous

18- Social

A2: Section 6 – Numerical Reasoning:

1- 100%

[(140-70) / 70] * 100 = 100%

2- 75%

[(1200-300) / 1200] * 100 = 75%

3- £ 33.6

£24 x 1.12 x 1.25 = £33.6

4- 5.5 Km/hr

(10x3 + 4x9) / 12 = 5.5 Km/hr

5- 15 Km

10 + 1 + 4 = 15Km

6- 30 Km/hr

15Km / 0.5 hours = 30 Km/hr

7- 96.25 Km/hr

440/4 = 110Km/hr. 110x7/8 = 96.25 Km /hour

8- 50

20 = x/0.4

X = 50

9- 1/5

12/60 = 1/5

10- 5400

¼ * 6 = 1.5 hours.

1.5 hours = 1.5x60x60 = 5400 seconds

11- Tuesday

12- 600 feet²

½ x 15 x 80

= 600

13- 20

14- 25 m²

Perimeter of square = 40 m .

Side of square = 40/4 = 10 m

Area of square = 10²= 100 m²

Perimeter of rectangle = 40 m

2 (length + width) = 40 m

2 (3Xwidth + width) = 40 m

width = 5 m and length = 15 m

Area of rectangle = 15 m X 5 m = 75 m²

Difference in Areas= 100 – 75 = 25 m²

15- 5 m

16- 10 years

s + 30 + 5 = 3 (s + 5)

17- 16m²

½ * 8 * 4 = 16m²

18- 64

19- 25

20- 1 day

21- 20%

22- 36

Series consists of squares of natural numbers.

23- 13

Series consists of prime numbers.

Exam B1

B1: Section 1 – Verbal Reasoning – Comprehension:

1- B

In the given passage, the minister says: "Your majesty, in my opinion, the royal elephant is not sick, but he his lonesome without his dear friend, the dog" (6th paragraph).

2- A

In 7th paragraph of the given passage, the minister says: "Your Majesty, make a declaration, that whoever has the dog that used to live at the royal elephant's shed will be penalized"

3- C

From the 4th paragraph it can be inferred that the elephant and the dog had become friends and when the dog was sold, the elephant became sad.

4- A

Refer to the 4th paragraph in which it is clearly written that the keeper sold the dog to an unknown man.

5- D

In the given context of the passage, the most suitable title of the passage is 'The bond of Friendship' as the passage emphasizes on the friendship of elephant and the dog.

6- C

Refer to 1st paragraph, "Elephant was very dear to the king, so he was well-fed and well-treated.

7- D

Refer to the second paragraph, "the dog could no longer **resist** the aroma of the rice and somehow managed to sneak into the elephant's shed"

8- D

Refer to the last paragraph, "As soon as he was freed, the dog ran back as fast as he could to the elephant's shed."

9- C

It is evident that the elephant-keeper sold the dog to a stranger despite it not belonging to him. Moreover, he was not at all concerned about the friendship between the elephant and the dog.The elephant-keeper, hence, was both greedy and insensitive.

10- A

It can be inferred from the passage that the king was compassionate and concerned about the elephant, but we cannot say for sure that he was an animal lover.

11- C

From the 7th paragraph, we can infer that the stranger became scared and that is why he set the dog free, because

he only did so after hearing the declaration of penalization by the king.

12- B

Refer to the last sentence of the passage, "rewarded the minister for his wise judgement"

13- A

Refer to the last paragraph, "The elephant was so delighted to see the dog that he picked his friend up with his trunk and swung him back and forth"

14- D

In the context of the passage, premises mean all the three words described above, hence correct option is D.

15- C

In the given context, the most similar word to 'Aroma' is 'Smell'

16- C

In the given context, the most similar word to 'Sneak' is to enter somewhere stealthily

17- C

In the given context, the most similar word to 'Extraction' is 'Received' or 'Gained'

18- C

In the given context, the most similar word to 'Declaration' is 'Announcement'

19- A

In the given context, the most opposite word to 'Resist' is 'Give in' that means to cease opposition.

20- D

In the given context, the most opposite word to 'Content' is 'Dissatisfied'

B1: Section 2 – Verbal Reasoning – Cloze:

1- World

Long ago people knew very little about the world

2- Earth

The earth was thought to be flat

3- Direction

If a person walked long enough in one direction

4- Edge

He would finally reach the edge of the world and fall off

5- Rectangular

Today we know that the earth is not a flat rectangular block

6- Round

It is round

7- Explorers

We owe this knowledge to the explorers

8- Voyages

who made long voyages to find new routes and discovered new lands

9- Oceans

They kept accurate records of the oceans they crossed

10- Map

They drew up the map of the world

11- Flat

In this way, they ended the belief of a flat world

12- Spirit

Though we know the earth much better today, the spirit of

13- Exploration

The spirit of exploration has, as a result, come to an end

14- Adventure

The desire for adventure

15- Curiosity

And the curiosity for far-flung places are still alive.

16- Besides

Besides, not all places on earth have been

17- Explored

Fully explored

18- Mountains

Places like deserts, mountains, oceans, and polar regions

19- Mysteries

Still have secrets and mysteries to amaze us

20- Discovered

It is fortunate for us that there are still many things to be discovered

21- Wonderful

That the earth remains rich and wonderful

B1: Section 3 – Verbal Reasoning – Odd One Out:

1- Cashew

Cashew is the only dry fruit

2- Bicycle

All others have engines

3- Fish

Fish only lives in water; the rest three can live on land as well as water

4- Shake

Other three are synonyms and refer to mixing

5- Pink

All others are colours of rainbow except pink

6- Brother

All others are females

7- Tap

All other can store water

8- Dam

Only dam is artificial, all others are natural

9- Obtuse

All others are types of triangles

10- Cube

All others are 2d shapes, whereas cube is 3d

11- June

Only June has 30 days, others have 31

12- Tennis

Only tennis is played with rackets.

13- Wolf

All others are pet animals

14- Grin

Grin has a positive connotation, whereas all others have a negative connotation.

15- Hideous

Hideous means ugly, other three are antonyms of hideous

16- Inch

All others are multiples of each other.

17- Clear

All other are antonyms of clear

18- Page

All others refer to writing.

B1: Section 4 – Verbal Reasoning – Antonyms:

1- Tiny

Enormous means very large, so its antonym is tiny

2- Terminated

Commissioned means enrolled, so its antonym is terminated

3- Natural

Artificial means man-made, so its antonym is natural

4- Influx

Exodus means 'going out' of large number of people, and influx means entry of the same, so they both are antonyms

5- Possess

Relinquish means to 'give up' on something, so its antonym is possess

6- Condense

Antonym of expand is condense

7- Immortal

Immortal is the opposite of mortal

8- Ordering

Obeying and ordering are opposites of each other

9- Genuine

Fraudulent means fake, deceitful, etc., so its antonym is genuine

10- Relaxed

Startled means 'alarmed', so its antonym is relaxed

11- Stale

Stale means not fresh, so fresh is the antonym of stale

12- Blameless

Culpable refers to someone who deserves blame, so opposite is blameless

13- Ignorant

Aware means to have knowledge of something, so ignorant is the opposite of this word

14- Expand

Shrink means to condense, so expand is the antonym

15- Rare

Rare is the antonym of common

16- Discomfort

Discomfort is the only correct word. Others are incorrect.

17- Frank

Evasive means cagey, so its antonym is frank

18- Antisocial

Gregarious means someone who is quite social, so antisocial is the antonym

B1: Section 5 – Non - Verbal Reasoning:

1- A

Shape 'A' is the only shape which is a rotated form of the big shape. All other shapes are flipped in some direction.

2- A

Shape 'A' is the only shape which is a rotated form of the big shape. All other shapes are flipped in some direction.

3- B

Shape 'B' is the only shape which is a rotated form of the big shape. All other shapes are flipped in some direction.

4- B

Shape 'B' is the only shape which is a rotated form of the big shape. All other shapes are flipped in some direction.

5- A

Shape 'A' is the only shape which is a rotated form of the big shape. All other shapes are flipped in some direction.

6- C

Shape 'C' is the only shape which is a rotated form of the big shape. All other shapes are flipped in some direction.

7- D

Shape 'D' is the only shape which is a rotated form of the big shape. All other shapes are flipped in some direction.

8- D

Shape 'D' is the only shape which is a rotated form of the big shape. All other shapes are flipped in some direction.

9- A

Shape 'A' is the only shape which is a rotated form of the big shape. All other shapes are flipped in some direction.

10- A

Shape 'A' is the only shape which is a rotated form of the big shape. All other shapes are flipped in some direction.

11- B

Shape 'B' completes the pattern of the shape on left.

12- B

Shape 'B' completes the pattern of the shape on left.

13- B

Shape 'b' completes the pattern of the shape on left.

14- C

Shape 'C' is the correct top-view of the 3d shape

15- A

Shape 'A' is the correct top-view of the 3d shape

16- B

Shape 'B' is the correct top-view of the 3d shape

17- B

Shape 'B' is the correct top-view of the 3d shape

18- A

Shape 'A' is the correct top-view of the 3d shape

Exam B2

B2: Section 1 – Numerical Reasoning:

1 a) 60

Total 4 baskets of apples. 4 baskets x 15 apples per basket = 60 apples

1 b)   420

Total baskets: 24

1/3rd baskets of oranges, 1/3 x 24 = 8 baskets of oranges.

Half baskets of guavas = 12 baskets of guavas

Remaining baskets of apples: 4 baskets of apples.

Total number of oranges = 8 baskets x 15 oranges per basket = 120 oranges

Total number of apples = 4 baskets x 15 apples per basket = 60 apples

Total number of guavas= 12 baskets x 20 guavas per basket = 240 guavas

So, total number of fruits = 120 + 60 + 240 = 420

1 c) 1 : 2 : 4

Apples : Oranges : Guavas = 60 : 120 : 240 = 1 : 2 : 4

1 d)   14.29%

Total no. of apples = 60

Total no. of fruits = 420

Probability of picking up an apple = 60/420   x   100%   =   14.2857%

2a) 7/103

Total number of cards = 52 + 51 = 103 (one ace is drawn out)

Total number of aces left = 7

Probability of picking up an ace = 7/103

2b) 25/103

Total number of cards = 103 (one card is already drawn out)

Total number of diamond cards = 13 + 12 = 25 (one ace of diamond is already drawn out)

Probability of picking up a diamond card = 25/103

2c) 1/2

Total no. of black cards = 52

Total no. of cards = 104

Probability of picking up a black card = 52/104 or ½

2d) 4/13

Total no. picture cards = 24

Total no. of ace cards = 8

Total no. of cards = 104

Probability of picking up an ace or picture card = 32/104 or 4/13

3a) 8,000,000 mm³

20cm = 20 x 10mm = 200 mm

0.40m = 0.40 x 1000mm = 400mm

Volume = 100mm x 200mm x 400mm = 8,000,000 mm³

3b) 2800 cm²

Surface area = 2 x (40 x 20)   +   2 x (10 x 20)   + 2 x (10 x 40)

= 1600 + 400 + 800

= 2800 cm²

3c) 8 litres

Volume of box in m³ = 0.4 x 0.2 x 0.1 = 0.008 m³

Amount of water in litres = 0.008m³ x 1000 litres = 8 litres

3d) 4 litres

Since 10 is half of 20, which is the total height, the volume of water will be half of the maximum volume.

Therefore Amount of water:

= 8/2

= 4 litres

4a) 0 cm²

DE=EC = 10 cm

Area of Δ AED = ½ X 10 X 10 = 50 cm²

Area of Δ BEC = ½ X 10 X 10 = 50 cm²

Difference = 50-50 = 0 cm²

4b) 100 cm²

Δ AEB has a height that is equal to the side of the rectangle = 10

Therefere Area

= ½ x 20 x 10

= 100 cm²

4c) 200cm², 60 cm

Area of rectangle = 20 x 10 = 200 cm²

Perimeter of rectangle = 20 + 20 + 10 + 10 = 60 cm

4d) 90°

Δ AED is an isosceles triangle (AD=DE). Therefore ∠AED = 45°

Δ BEC is an isosceles triangle (BC=EC). Therefore ∠BEC = 45°

∠AED + ∠AEB + ∠BEC = 180° (Angle at a point)

Therefore 45° + ∠AEB + 45° = 180°

∠AEB = 90°

5a) £0.50

Selling price of 50-pages notebook = £1.50

Cost on 50 pages notebook = £0.50 + 0.1x50 = £1.00

Profit on 50-pages notebook = = £1.50 - £1.00 = £0.50

5b) £0.25

Selling price of 75-pages notebook = £2.00

Cost of 75 pages notebook = £0.50 + 0.1x75 = £1.25

Profit on 75-pages notebook = £2.00 - £1.25 = = £0.75

Selling price of 100 pages notebook = £2.50

Cost of 100 pages notebook = = £0.50 + 0.1x100 = £1.50

Profit on 100 pages notebook = = £2.50 - £1.50 = £1.00

Value of extra profit on 100 pages notebook as compared to the 75 pages notebook = £1.00 - £0.75 = £0.25

5c) £23.00

Profit on 50 pages notebooks = 15 x £0.50 = £7.50

Profit on 75 pages notebooks = 10 x £0.75 = £7.50

Profit on 100 pages notebooks = 8 x £1.00 = £8.00

TOTAL PROFIT = £7.50 + £7.50 + £8.00 = £23.00

5d) £2.00

Profit on 100 pages notebook = £1.00

Cost of 50 pages notebook = £1.00

So the selling price of 50 pages notebook needs to be £2.00 in order for the profit to be equal to that of 100 pages notebook

6a) 20 KM

The vertical axis shows 20KM reading corresponding to the last point of the graph line.

6b) Resting

Between 20-30 minutes, the distance is not increasing, hence it can be inferred that Danny is resting during that time.

6c) 30-42 minutes

The graph has maximum steepness in this region, which shows that the speed is maximum here.

6d) 42-60 minutes

In this interval, the steepness of graph is the minimum.

7a) £2.5 million

Total amount = £ 10 million

Laura's share = 20% = 20/100 x £10 million = £2 million

Tom's share = 1/10 = 1/10 x £10 million = £1million

Sara's share = 2/5 = 2/5 x £10million = £4 million

John's share = 0.5 million

Michael's share = £10million - £2million - £1million - £4million - £0.5million =
= £2.5million

7b) Sara

Sara gets the highest amount of money (4 million) as determined in the last part

7c) 5%

John's share = 0.5million / 10 million x 100 = 5%

7d) £0.1 million or £100,000

John's share = 5%

John's share in extra £2 million = 5/100 x £2 million = £0.1 million or £100,000

8a) 64 °C

The temperature if falling by 6°C every minute, hence after 6 minutes, the temperature would be 64°C

8b) 100 – 6n

6°C is falling every minute, so the expression is 100 – 6n

8c) 12 minutes

After 12 minutes, temperature is = 100 – 6(12) = 28°C. Hence 12 mins are required.

9a) 30°

x = 90° - 60° (BFG is right angled triangle)

Now, Triangle AFG, sum of angles = 180. So, angle 'a' = 180 – 90 - 60 = 30°

9b) 45°

y = 15° (BFE is right angled triangle, so 45+30+y = 90°, so y=15°)

Now, Triangle CFE, sum of angles = 180. So, d= 180-90 – 15 – 30 = 45°

9c) 75°

Consider triangle DEF, sum of angles = 180.

So, f = 180 – 90 – 15 = 75°

9d) 15°

Explanation as given above in

10a)   25 years

Let daughter's age = d

Let man's age = 2d

25 years' ago, the man's age would be

2d – 25 and since he was 25 year old then;

18

2d – 25 = 25

d = 25

So present age of daughter = 25 years

10b)   25 years

After 25 years, the daughter would be 50 years old while the man would be 75 years old, hence the daughter will be 50/75 = 2/3rd of his age.

11a)   8

No. of girls = 1/5 x 40 = 8

11b)   36

No. of boys = 40 – 8 = 32

Half of the girls are above 5 feet. i.e. 4 girls

So total no. of pupils who are above 5 feet tall = 32+4= 36

12a)   22

2 full circles + one 3/4th of circle. So, total = 8 + 8 + 6 = 22

12b)   12

1 full circle and a half circle = 8 + 4 = 12

12c)   6

No. of people who eat cereals =6 + 6 = 12

No. of people who eat boiled eggs = 6

Difference = 12 – 6 = 6

12d)   60

Total no. of people = 8+8+6+8+4+6+6+6+4+4 = 60

13a)   16 feet

Let length = 2x, width = x

So,

$$2x.x = 128$$

$$2x^2 = 128$$

$$x^2 = 64$$

$$x = 8 \text{ ft}$$

Now, length = 2x = 2(8) = 16 ft

13b)   8 feet

Explanation given above

13c)   40 feet

Length of boundary wall = 16 + 16 + 8 = 40 feet

14a)   £5.00

Cost = £4.00 (extra-large size) + £0.25+£0.25 (2 basic toppings) + £0.50 (one special topping) = £5.00

14b)   £3.95

Cost = £3.20 (medium size) + £0.25 (one basic topping) + £0.50 (one special topping) = £3.95

14c) £7.25

Maximum Cost = £4.00 (extra- large size) + £0.25 x 5 (5 basic toppings) + £0.50 x 5 (5 special toppings) = £7.25

14d) £2.40

Discounted Cost = £2.50 x 0.8 (small size, 20% discount) + £0.25 x 0.6 (one basic topping with 40% discount) + £0.50 x 0.5 (special topping with 50% discount) = £2.40

B2: Section 2 – Verbal Reasoning – Cloze:

1- Unlike

Unlike other insects which live alone

2- Together

These bees live together in what is known as a bee colony

3- Rest

She is larger than the rest of the bees

4- In

Her main task in the colony is to lay eggs

5- Collect

These bees collect nectar and pollen from the flowers

6- Into

Converted into honey

7- After

The worker bees also help look after the younger bees

8- Hatched

As soon as the eggs are hatched

9- With

The worker bees feed the young bees with pollen and nectar

10- Such

The main task of such a bee is to mate with new queen

11- Span

The queen bee has a life span of about three years

12- Laid

During this period, she would have laid more than half a million eggs

13- When

When the queen bee is dying, a new queen would be groomed

14- Latter

The new queen would eventually take over the 'duties' of the older queen when the old queen dies

1- A

Shape 'A' is the correct top-view of the 3d shape

2-   A

Shape 'A' is the correct top-view of the 3d shape

3-   D

Shape 'D' is the correct top-view of the 3d shape

4-   C

Shape 'C' is the correct top-view of the 3d shape

5-   C

Shape 'C' is the correct top-view of the 3d shape

6-   A

Shape 'A' is the correct top-view of the 3d shape

7-   A

Shape 'A' is the correct top-view of the 3d shape

8-   C

Shape 'C' is the correct top-view of the 3d shape

9-   A

Shape 'A' is the correct top-view of the 3d shape

10- C

Shape 'C' is the correct top-view of the 3d shape

11- A

Shape 'A' is the only rotated shape of the big shape. All other shapes are flipped in some direction.

12- A

Shape 'A' is the only rotated shape of the big shape. All other shapes are flipped in some direction or different shapes than the original.

13- A

Shape 'A' is the only rotated shape of the big shape. All other shapes are flipped in some direction.

14- A

Shape 'A' is the rotated shape. The rest are different than the original shape.

15- A

Shape 'A' is the only rotated shape of the big shape. All other shapes are flipped in some direction.

16- A

Shape 'A' is the only rotated shape of the big shape. All other shapes are flipped in some direction

Printed in Great Britain
by Amazon

79741352R00086